Spittle

ISBN: 978-1-913642-45-7

Book designed by Aaron Kent

Edited by Aaron Kent

Broken Sleep Books (2021), Talgarreg, Wales

Contents

Andrew Kötting, HUB BUB IN THE BAOBABS *(1989)*

Light Glyphs:
Collected Interviews

David Spittle

Rushes to Frame , an introduction

1.

I had written –

Stan Brakhage referred to his own films as 'filmpoems', a term informed by his dedicated reading of the poets Robert Duncan, Charles Olson, William Carlos Williams, Ezra Pound, Louis Zukofsky, Robert Creeley, Michael McClure and Ronald Johnson. Brakhage considered his films to be 'visual ineffables' that could re-invigorate meaning outside of language, hot-wired back into the nervous system. Fingers pressing on the eyelids, to see the eye – a magma of the body's light.

Movement and colour that confounds reference, a visual flow or shape that cannot be described in language but instead forces new understandings of what a language might be: the 'un-nouned' communication of 'light-glyphs'.

Maya Deren put forward a distinction between the <u>horizontal </u>and vertical ‖‖ in film.

The horizontal embodied the linear development of plot, presented and experienced over sequential time, the vertical embodied the suspended exploration of associations that co-exist in a moment.

I wanted to offer ways into this suspended exploration, in moments where poetry contests/interrupts /distracts/interacts with /distorts/ intervenes/contorts/screens/ the element we label film

The Text of Light

or where film influences/enters/ exhumes/directs/challenges/resurrects/ collects/ rejects/ attracts/ emits/admits/ and fits the element we label poetry

The Light of Text

Light Glyphs: poets on film / filmmakers on poetry

2.

Notes from –

> A
> Circular window opens
> a clouding

where LIKE is lyric 'I' to subject as LENS is seeing 'eye' to object

neither speaking on behalf but half of speaking out of nowhere

a while back, in 2015, when any I that was was 26, studying
John Ashbery & Surrealism   reading at a Cine/Poem event
organised by SJ Fowler   I   was   trying to say

a gesture of mistranslation from language to light, reversed
from image to text, frame word to frame, page to screen, and as
screen as page and film as poetry and back to poetry as film.

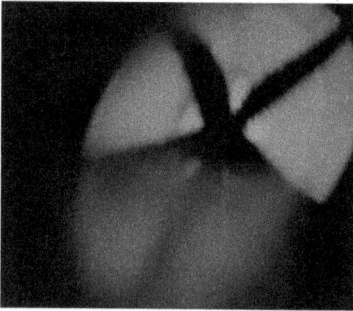

looking back   *in {the} cut*
grammar of how rhythm
            from
a position of vague drifts

'For time is an emulsion, and probably thinking not to
        grow up
 Is the brightest kind of maturity for us' **Ashbery**

a crouched audience in a small gallery
poets & filmmakers & the lost, lost, lost

3.

On the next page

into a shared communion of sleep
overhead the beam, how dreaming
holds a torch and   *the screen*   *is held*

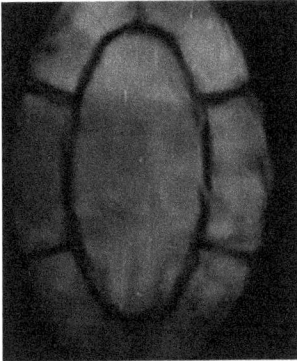

whose other time enacts its daily stroll
whose minutes wake the clock
with actors to resume its role
pick up from where life last left off
and take the light in thirsty gulps
of film and air and always there
rehearse the flickered day

L'Etoile de Mer (Man Ray, 1928)   **i**   **began**

writing a poem, 'Light Noise'
sit me in a dark, dark room. this daring future
passing on the tracks.
i'm the fellow who lost the watch and yes, they used to be like children

after finding   *between*

he keeps a diary. he forgets to write.
to make a modus operandi of moving in the dark.
slender arms and paperweights. nocturnal tread on perfect lawns

my dead grandfather's 8mm reels   A
                                        Circular window opens
                                        a clouding
O
          silhouettes (a
starfish as it turns   handwritten
the seen   *M a n R a y*   who   in describing
Desnos' poem   said   'There was no dramatic action,
                yet all the elements for a possible action.'

imagining

I don't need the living ones. nobody answers – **Alzheimer's**
the wires have been cut. but you don't want to live alone, do you?
it's too late for that. the leaf as it fell. we will be children again.

in the film's decay

4.

i looked through my notes made on starting *Light Glyphs* in 2015:

For the surrealist Louis Aragon, film could 'endow with a poetic value that which does not yet possess it'. What that 'poetic value' might be endures as a shifting and various tension throughout film history and our changing experiences of watching film. This is not to condemn 'poetic value' to the icky sentimentalism of some non-specific beauty. It is not to evoke 'poetry' as, and in, complacent shorthand; and not to blandly perform the same woolly qualification as 'arty' in the task of roughly gesticulating where description fails.

Breton found the poetry of cinema in its ability to confuse, an experience beyond rational or functional sense: 'I think what we valued most in it, to the point of taking no interest in anything else, was its power to disorient.' Leaving one film to dive into another, walking in and out of films, dizzying ends into beginnings and refusing the direction of narrative.

i remember telling a poet who I really admired how much I'd like to write academically about their work, they replied: 'don't do that – let's collaborate.'

Poetry in film's ability to disarrange and undo, a sitting in the dark to be with light adopting the unconscious in conscious thought; being consciously adopted by the unconscious

up from the desk, out of the house, reach out to, listen and see, to learn from those who inspired; these were some of the reasons.

Ado Kyrou, 'learn to go and see the "worst" films they are sometimes sublime'

Background sets that breathe with more conviction than the actors

Film ignites / invites poetic reading against the grain of its intentions. Film should not have to be read nor poetry seen for either to imagine in / as / from / for

after finishing the Phd and entering the cursory years of 'freelance' unemployment –the juggling meanderings of now, to continue –

collaboration and conversation has more to offer; to lend poetry a practical intelligence, vagrant ways to embody.

Tarkovsky understood poetry as beyond literary definition, existing in and as the indiscernible movements of being, beyond coherent logic. For Tarkovsky, the indiscernible movement of being is time. Film, as the medium best equipped to render time was for him consequently the perfect art of poetry.

For Joseph Cornell, squirrelling away his constellated objects in the basement of Utopia Parkway, re-purposing forgotten film-reels and preserving the trace of moments in boxed kingdoms: "It is not the carefully composed images but rather their ultimate relationship to each other that generates the poetic connection".

      use a feather to cross-index a mythology of flight

and then, Rose Hobart
                blue nocturnes feverish
                collage East of Borneo

midnight obsessively spliced in glances, a submerged lunar quality

the significance of looking again

I include these notes

only because, at the time, these scraps of excitable half-thought and study were kindling – beginnings of discovery – that both film and poetry could be explorations into, and as, *ways of meaning* and *ways of seeing*; alive in (and to) the fluid interactions of what is visual, semantic, and textual. It was a sense of *moving* into the formulations of meaning as they undulate in and out of sight, consciousness, or comprehension.

Meaning without the monopolising referents, messages, and narrative of what is meant. Films and poems that interrupt or lay bare how we structure our modes of understanding; to enact the structuring itself. How it reaches us, a beam of light to a screen, a thought that exchanges its position as thought for thinking's positionality. All manner of fancifully pseudo-academic confabulations that – as it turns out – really needed to be nailed down and clarified…but I was drawn on to further convolutions, as nudged forward by Ashbery's poetry and Surrealism. These led me into wanting to better understand phenomenology. I felt Surrealism was – at its most compelling – an application of such intensity to attention, that waking life became more and more dreamlike. Not in whimsical surprise or violent parataxis but in a slow filtering through of a different colour or vibrancy to observation… similar to emerging from a cinema, blinking into the too-bright-sky and feeling gratefully – and often mysteriously – changed. Not an eruption of the dream (and Breton's 'Convulsive Beauty') but the realisation that if we attend to our own attention and grasp the texture of experience as its own experience – in the experiential *how* we look and not the referential *what* that is looked at – consequently, whatever constitutes and guides our relationship with reality can begin to change

The confluence of Surrealism and Ashbery as it led me into film –

the articulation of experience and the experience of articulation.

The strange foam, depths, and shallows;

rinsing small-talk in the glitter or

heavily descending like whales through ink.

A straining writer's metaphor

as its vehicle greedily overtakes the tenor

and how inane, how gnomic those transmissions

as they turn over

themselves

to nest in white noise, murmuring

erasures

promising to return.

That first film,

or, as Ashbery's poem, 'Soonest Mended',

so peacefully ends –

to begin again,

'To the mooring of starting out, that day so long ago'.

And there is a part of me, a whatever I that was, that feels a distant irritation at twice quoting from one of his most famous poems… as opposed to more adventurous tracts. But those memories (of my research + obsessive reading of JA), as important as they are to me, have opened up to their own spongey disappearances. I haven't properly, deeply, read Ashbery's poetry since 2016, on finishing the PhD. It was not because I didn't want to, but that I feel I am still wandering through its pleasant mist…and that now, it simply being there, and having had the privilege to spend time with it, keeps emanating its own assurance – the airborne radio tuned between stations.

More significantly, in a moment when planets aligned and my writing-life prematurely peaked, I was able to meet Ashbery in New York – where we talked film, and later, he kindly agreed to the interview in this book. We met in 2014, three years before his death. I feel a real longing to convey how much his poetry changed my life, and continues to…but in those moments, trying to talk about it feels like intruding on memories and feelings that I want to protect. It helps to turn instead to his poetry, in another of his beginnings, from *Three Poems*:

> I thought that if I could put it all down, that would be one way. And next the thought came to me that to leave all out would be another, and truer, way.

What Ashbery and Surrealism opened up to me was a world within a world, as a result of seeing this world anew; to be found in the movements *between* that somehow cohere

– the flicker that lends each frame its motion.

It was also the welcome blur of any distinction or polarity from which to hang the bridge of 'between'. Instead, onto a *moving* that necessarily confused the *one* or *other* in the surrealist dictum of 'one in the other'; a kinetic mobility and fluidity of , and as, perception (or do I *mean* seeing or speech or listening or writing or reading or all as they mix into being?). There are better ways of defining this, but rather than insist on definition, my enthusiasm was closer to the 'possible action' that Man Ray found in Desnos' poem. Not one thing, not 'one' and not 'thing' but what awakes *as* correspondence that was previously only noticed *in* correspondence.

Finding those rhythms of perception, and the attendant or resulting versions of meaning, as embodied in poetry and film, was what led to talking more to artists/filmmakers/poets/ writers working in this fluid and 'possible action'. To pursue in conversation.

5.

I include these notes, from now and then

because on re-reading these interviews, not only am I struck by
how much has changed in this stridently sinking island (the not
so U of K) and (as ever) in poetry and film – but also how my own
writing has changed. Not that I'd want to tiresomely elaborate on
that, but I had to stop myself from editing – as I thought that, in
the spirit of capturing / recording, it was best to leave things as
they were.

I have focused on Ashbery and Surrealism for this introduction,
not in neglect of all the wonderful filmmakers and poets in this
book but because, for me, that was where the impulse to make
these interviews began. That, and Guy Maddin...

The never departing and always leaving trains, the sleep,
cartographies of snow, crackling signals from disappearing streets;
dreams of family, mythologized in a haunted city symphony
where hockey-players and hairdressers raise the keys to long gone
addresses and a winter keeps horses frozen up to their necks
and held (like Eadweard Muybridge's 'Sallie Gardner' caught
mid-gallop, suspended) like scattered chess pieces; all forgetting,
muttering, turning in a sleepless dream of waking, circling in
memory as it snows outside, and the glow in-front of a family
television with its own snowy reception...drifts

my first viewing of *My Winnipeg* (2007)...

...moving back into the soviet-style montage miracle of *The Heart
of the World* (2000), and then on again through his 'Me-Trilogy'
with *Cowards Bend the Knee* (2003), the incredible peep-show
of crazed psychoanalysis and its fertile confabulations...digging
into the lost language of Silent Cinema, a discarded vocabulary
of gesture and light brought reeling back but not, significantly,
through nostalgia but instead a rupturing vitality; the abandoned
and anarchic roots of an art that were cut short in favour of tech-
nological change, conjured and called back to interrogate, incant,
and reanimate...throughout Maddin's filmography, histories

of early cinema are denied any historical distance and brought into the feverish humour and heartbreak of trying to understand *now*.... invoked through séance, in the melancholy sleepwalkers of remembering, of catharsis, dream and confession...

...into *Brand upon the Brain!* (2006) and the roving eye of a maternal lighthouse, child detectives, a reanimated corpse, and such restless and restlessly imaginative flights of narrative...or back to Bolshevik amnesia in *Archangel* (1990) recalling the ornately crowded set design in Josef Von Sternberg's films... the Robert Walser inflected Mountain movie, *Careful* (1992), with its trembling colours...a vampiric ballet that recalls early Buñuel in *Dracula: Pages from a Virgin's Diary* (2002)...or, the first Maddin film I saw in the cinema, the surrealist noir comedy of *Keyhole* (2011), a film that brings desire and memory, and all infringements and coalescing shadows therein, into a labyrinth of strange homecomings for what is the strangest labyrinth of all, the home ... and, in *The Forbidden Room* (2015), epic exfoliations of narrative decay & bloom into and out of each other like the eccentric and meticulous writing of Raymond Roussel, a film where Maddin collaborated with Ashbery – who wrote the mischievously framing outer-onion layer to this expansive reverie of stories and storytellers... told with all poetic blemishes intact...

Without Guy Maddin I wouldn't have learnt to revel in cinema as occult amnesia, as delirious fog...I wouldn't have had initiation into the mad poetry in Abel Gance, Louis Feuillade, Carl Dreyer, G.W. Pabst, Eric Von Stroheim, Jean Vigo, Georges Franju, Tod Browning, Alexander Dovzhenko, Von Sternberg & Marlene Dietrich... leaping into the queasy confections and welling melodrama of Douglas Sirk... ways of inhaling films, nitrate swamps that kindly beget their own intoxications in an appetite for searching that, though it might leave Maddin's path, will always be formatively inspired by *his way of seeing*.

The feeling after I'd watched the Quay Brother's uniquely somnambulant, *Institute Benjamenta* (a film that united both Maddin and Ashbery's passions)...or after seeing Nobuhiko Ôbayashi's deliriously colourful *Hausu*; or the folkloric macabre of Rainer Sarner's astounding *November*, or Juraj Herz's *The*

Cremator, Vêra Chytilová's *Fruit of Paradise*, Bill Morrison's *Decasia*...no dates...just films circling the vast spill of cinematic time. The eye of the whale in *Werkmeister Harmonies*...the psychotronic lunacy and ambition of Teruo Ishi's *Horrors of Malformed Men....* Proustian decadence in Zoltán Huszárik's *Szinbád*, Pere Portabelo, Jack Smith, Peter Strickland, Jan Švankmajer, Pedro Costa, Jonas Mekas, Andrea Luka Zimmerman, Paul Leni, Oscar Micheaux, F. Percy Smith, Lucrecia Martel, Abigail Child... everything in conversation; threading together, intruding on each other's dreaming, dissolved into, greeting, arguing...the frenzied stuttering of Jeff Keen's flaming montage...the gentle wisdom of Margaret Tait as it imbibes the landscape and stands by the sea... meditative reincarnations in Michelangelo Frammartino's *Le Quattro Volte...* wings in water and fish in sky, Lucien Castaing-Taylor and Véréna Paravel's *Leviathan*...Jacques Tati, Wojciech Has, Nathaniel Dorsky... *Mothlight* shown before *Mothra*... Ingmar Bergman and Herschel Gordon Lewis discuss the soul and its splatter as Buster Keaton dives into the balletic ocean of Jean Painlevé's *The Love Life of the Octopus*, whilst onlookers take out their phones to watch another trailer for a film they won't remember...I only haphazardly list directors and films as this was how I often encountered them...in other interviews with Maddin, I gratefully pored over his references to films as they became cherished coordinates to keep searching, seeing, exhuming, invoking and maybe, with a misty contentment, to sink into their narcotic warp and sleep.

INTERTITLE READS:

                      MUST LEAVE THE DARK ROOM

INTERTITLE READS:

                      WATCH YOUR STEP

INTERTITLE READS:

                      WHO SAW WHO AND WHEN AND

The chance to have ways of thinking, writing and seeing opened to new and changing possibilities, and to equally recognise – in thought, language, and light – where our limits can be re-imagined as generative: where cognition ends and intuition or awareness emanates instead; where codes of language fall short and cracked speech, gaps, slips and the incomprehensible, the typographic, spatial, obscured, oblique, absent and erased, when these reassert meaning's variety; as shadow, or in where the light escapes and how it obscures, in what is missing from the frame or smudging the lens.

I would like to express my immense gratitude to all who took part – for the generosity of their insight and the ongoing inspiration of their work.

INTERTITLE READS:

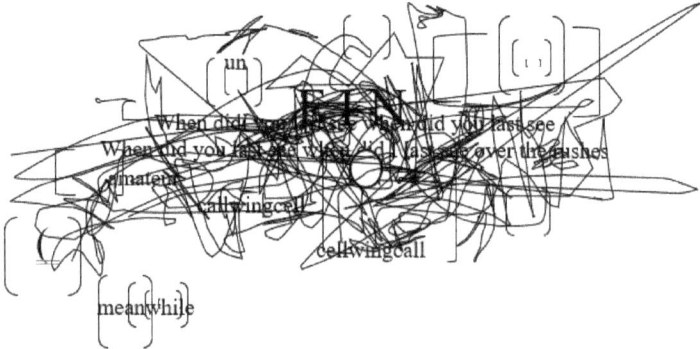

GUY MADDIN

To be able to begin the 'Light Glyph' series of interviews with Canadian filmmaker Guy Maddin is a real privilege. There exists no better inauguration than to dive into the ideas and perambulations of one of modern cinema's most inventive, entertaining and consistently original practitioners. His films itch and explode with the busy extravagance of Josef Von Sternberg, yearn with the aching melodramas of Douglas Sirk and libidinously exhume the spirit of early Luis Buñuel. Adopting the orphaned and outmoded in cinema's history, as digested by his own humour and obsessions, Maddin quarries a lovingly warped archaeology of film with which to ferment and reinvent personal mythologies. The near-occult dynamics of family and the primacy of childhood become points of ritual, never far from troubled or vulnerable desire and, as all else in Maddin's foggy cartography, encountered most frequently in and as memory.

Though his filmography demonstrates recurrent themes and aesthetic preferences, he has nevertheless accumulated a diverse body of work: from the midnight-movie, cult success of *Tales from Gimli Hospital* (1988), a film that had critics equivocating between allusions to *Eraserhead*, Man Ray and John Waters, to the labyrinthine ambition of his latest feature *The Forbidden Room* (2015). *The Forbidden Room* is a propulsive, vast and hall ucinatory feat of of narrative; like a Russian-doll raconteur evoking the writing of Raymond Roussel, it features an 'outer-onion' framing device scripted by the American poet John Ashbery. Ashbery has often cited Maddin's *The Saddest Music in the World* (2003) as a favourite film, and, in addition to admiring each other's work, they also shared a recent collage exhibition (2015) at the Tibor de Nagy gallery, New York.

In this interview I wanted to ask Maddin about aspects of this poetic collaboration and to hear more about his own relationship with poetry. It was also a chance to consider the visual manipulation, newly explored with co-director Evan Johnson, in digital form. Outside of its own innovation in digital film, *The Forbidden Room* was also accompanied by a pioneering online incarnation, *Séances* (2015). *Séances* is an interactive project based on a method of 'algorithmic storytelling', allowing viewers to 'conjure' filmic episodes (some of which appear in *The Forbidden Room*) whereby each viewing witnesses a uniquely sequenced and un-repeatable composition. Every film, on ending becomes a 'lost film', bringing the creative process back to its origin which, for Maddin, was the re-imagining of lost films. Those buried or burnt reels, the mouldering moulding and hidden histories that shadow our conception of cinema history with its own murky double: a forgotten cinema that, through neglect, erasure, or damage, enacts its own forgetting through the chemical distortions of celluloid.

Maddin's interest in movements between presence and absence in film, each constantly haunted by the other, draws his cinema towards an innately poetic dynamic. Obsessions caught in the ghost traffic of memory. When and where what we see and say drops off, desire and dreaming begin to speculatively unfurl – these movements (between presence and absence, loss and retrieval) allow Maddin's cinema to orbit its own ghosts, alternating between wandering melancholy and exultant mischief ; to sleepwalk through snow, through chance encounters, dreamy collisions and séance, and to arrive drowsily at the door of an address that is no longer yours – keys from a past life turning in the lock.

DS

*I know that Michael Silverblatt [**interviewer and host of KCRW Bookworm**] introduced you to John Ashbery but I wondered whether there were ever any other poetic discoveries that have become comparably important for you? In the tradition of George Toles [academic and collaborating writer] and Michael's chaperoned book guides (**and like the loving and solemn ritual of a mixtape between friends**) if you were to compose a list of poetry recommendations, what might be on it?*

GM

Well, I like the prose poetry, if that's what it is, of De Chirico's *Hebdomeros*. And I like Jules Laforgue's *Moralités légendaires* (1887), which contains prose poetry biographies of Hamlet, Salome, Perseus and Andromeda, and Lohengrin. I love the prose too of Osip Mandelstam – his *Egyptian Stamp* is the best.

Maybe it's just prose, not even prose poetry -- who can tell, because now I'm thinking of how much I love Pasternak's *Safe Conduct*, which is just prose, though redolent of poesy! Gimme the prose of Nerval and Mallarmé, -- did Mallarmé even write any prose? -- and, um, Frederick Seidel. He's a poet! I guess I love prose that yanks the rug out from under my feet and leaves me floating somewhere. For that reason, I also love Ezra Pound's apparent complete rewrite-within-a-translation of Paul Morand's *Open All Night*. I know these don't all add up to Ashbery, but I love them all and Ashbery too. Silverblatt and Toles both guided me through the first decades of my reading. The stories Michael recommended that most affected me were the Beckett novels and Flann O'Brien's *At-Swim-Two-Birds*. I love this latter book so much it hurts. I can't believe it took me thirty years to read O'Brien's *The Third Policeman*, which might be one of my top five favourite books of all time. Or top fifty, now that I think of it, but top, way up there – so dreamy-dream-dreamy!

DS

The shared Tibor de Nagy exhibition of your collages with Ashbery's seemed like such a natural and exciting match, at what point did you start sharing your collages with Ashbery?

GM

I can't remember if I ever showed him any. I was a longtime fan of his, and I must have showed him something because he suggested I approach the Tibor with my stuff – but I never did! Wait, no, I did! I ran some of my stuff in the *Sienese Shredder*, a fantastic arts annual put out by Ashbery friends Brice Brown and Trevor Winkfield. I was so proud to be included among the artists who peopled its pages. There was stuff by Ron Padgett, James Schuyler, Jasper Johns – and me! Ridiculous! Then one day I just got an invitation from the director of Tibor asking me – no, telling me – I had a joint show with Ashbery at the gallery if I wished. Just send in some collage, Guy! I didn't have any left, so I had to host a few collage parties to get some made. I know Ashbery always works on his scissoring and gluing alone, but I always do it in social situations. I get lonely easily and nothing comes! So I bought some wine and cheese, and some new LPs, and soon I was happily crafting the crap out of some old magazines until I had my share for the show done.

*Your collages from around the period of **Keyhole**, like the film itself, seemed darker and more psychosexual than your later collages in the Tibor exhibition. How much was the change in style a reaction to the different tone of **The Forbidden Room** and **Séances**, and how much was influenced by Ashbery's collages and the nature of your collaboration?*

Ashbery had a huge influence on me. I love how his collage work is often the result of just one move, just one image combined with another to form a new visual meaning or some kind of delight. He made me simplify my collage. Also, with *Keyhole* in the past, my mood brightened considerably. In recent months my collages are almost exclusively in colour. I hate to supply reductive reasons but my life seems happier and more stable now, plus I decided to challenge myself with the formidable task of contriving palettes for the work. I went to the paint store and asked for one of their "colour complement" wheels and made the new work with that wheel by my side all the time, for handy complement double-checking.

I'm now hooked on colour, and making things pretty, and putting one thing on top of another. The whole world is a collage, or so it seems now, and everyone in it is Ashberian, or everyone is a part of speech in Ashbery's singular vernacular! Now I see everything that delights me in terms of the component parts of a collage, the unlikely collision of two things, sounds, events, flavours. I'm especially into the titles randomly generated by the program running *Séances* – at the end of each viewing experience a film cemetery of titles created and lost by this site is listed. If you sit through a movie and take screen-captures you'll find a fairly high batting average of near-Ashberian charm. It's up to the reader to impose his own Ashberian qualities onto these things, but I swear they're there! Also, I love what-if collages involving one musician, a long-dead one, doing a cover of a song written since their death. I can go on forever with this one. I really want to hear Leadbelly covering ScHoolboy Q's "Big Body." I want Nat King Cole to sing "King Kunta"! You know, it can't happen, it never will, but it MUST!

DS

Could you say a bit about Ashbery's script for his collage-play, **The Inn of the Guardian Angel** *(according to the questionable omnipotence of Wikipidea, this was given to you by Ashbery, and is collaged from New York Times obituaries and Hollywood fanzines...it sounds amazing!)*

GM

The play is an incredible piece of writing. Not to mention type-writing! It's 83-pages long, typed, single-spaced, and it's all Ash-bery. I think wiki got it as right as I did. I think I'm even the source for that wiki entry – how often do you find someone willing to admit he's the source for a wiki entry? From what I recall John told me he collaged the play together from obituaries and fanzines, but my memory is terrible, and who knows how much he was spoon-feeding me with his explanation – I'm only a filmmaker, I spend all my time stressing to John how much of an outsider I am when it comes to poetry. John generously included the rights to film *The Inn of the Guardian Angel* along with our legal document giving me the right to shoot his adaptation of the lost Dwain Esper film *How to Take a Bath*, which we shot way back in the summer of 2010 and then later included as the framing structure that held , sort of held, together our 2015 feature film *The Forbidden Room*. Esper was a sexploitationist who also shot *Reefer Madness* and *How to Undress in Front of Your Husband*. He also took over the distribution of Tod Browning's *Freaks* when the film was banned. So in 1937 he made a film with the titillating title, *How to take a Bath*. It apparently compared how married and unmarried women bathed – that's when the word spinster was still used on driver's licenses to describe the unmarried. Anyway, I think the married bathed with much more lubricity, while the spinsters' soapsuds lacked the nacre. I picture the whole thing in split screen, a great excuse for Esper's art department to pile suds just so high on the chest of an actress. John's adaption is a total rewrite. I love it so, and I'm so proud to have his words in our feature. Wow. I wish John wrote screenplays more often. I love his plays, which are hard to get – what's that one of his adapted from a *Rin-Tin-Tin* movie, but with humans playing and speaking the roles of the dogs? So dreamy! I have it somewhere in my apartment, or one of my subletters took it. Things are always disappearing around here! I begged John, shamelessly, to write more screenplays for me, but to get rid of me he sent me this *Inn of the Guardian Angel*. Every day during the 2010 production of my feature *Keyhole* I had actors read aloud from the *Inn* while I video-recorded them. It was so difficult for the actors to understand the play, to give the lines any welcoming sense they were understood. Mind you, some of these actors were having trouble with their normal lines, and most of them enjoyed it far too much whenever I read the morning paper out loud to them during hair and make-up.

DS

Starting with **Keyhole** *and certainly continuing in* **The Forbidden Room** *and in the* **Seances** *project, it seems like more horror inflected elements are entering the Maddin universe... would you agree? Obviously we're not talking unequivocal 'genre' horror, but I feel with some of the new visual techniques you're exploring and alongside a constant interest in hauntings, and altered, delirious, trance-like or frenzied states, more eerie moments are appearing...*

GM

I wish I were working in genres. I'd be doing myself a favour, from the funding point of view anyway. Man, I was always so proud of being described as sui generis, genre-free, but I was proud of something that was screwing me over completely. I might as well have been proud of being the most financially unsuccessful, or the most impossible to sell, filmmaker of them all. What a maroon! But I am delirious, always delirious, obsessed with my own amnesias. I connected with amnesia plots in melodrama and soap operas even in childhood, and believe me I wasn't thinking in analytic terms back then. They just hit me. I guess I've always had the kind of dreams while sleeping that stayed with me long into the day, the feelings they produced anyway, and for as long as I can remember I've dreamt about things I missed the most. I'd dream about my dead brother come alive, my dead Chihuahua come alive, my dead grandmother, dad and Aunt Lil. All of them got regularly restored to me in my sleep. The cottage at the lake, which I was only taken to in the summer would be restored to me all winter long, and the happy feelings they produced in me would stay with me well into the day, past lunchtime sometimes. I saw these dreams as a forgetting. I'd forgotten all the funerals, the deaths. I'd forgotten it was no longer summer, at least while I was sleeping. I'd forgotten people were dead, and the feelings of seeing them again, that's what I remembered. In a way, forgetting is not just the flip side of remembering, but an important part of remembering. I'd forget one thing, the absence, and that would permit me dream access to the memories of things long removed from me. It was like getting handed a telescope in my sleep, so I could see and feel things up close I would never be able to conjure up as simple daytime memories, not without the vividness of dreams. Conversely, by day I've always been a stupefied cotton-headed groper through waking life, always forgetting the most serious problems pressing, really pressing, for real, in on me. I'd forget to do homework, forget to do chores around the house, forget the time as it passed in front of the TV. I'd forget as a young man I was a father, and fall short in my duties there. As a young father I'd frequently forget my wedding vows, forget to file taxes, forget my manners. Mix all that up with my bumper crop of dream amnesias and I was one confused person, I don't know how I got across the street, so befuddled was I, and remain to this day, so frequently getting my feet tangled up in memories, always flipping back and forth between past and present, never involving the future in my intoxicated reveries. Yes, I was drunk on such reveries, obsessions with the past, almost a sublime connoisseur of the past's flavours as they mingle with the present's. I learned later Falkner believed the past and the present exist simultaneously, "the past ain't even past" or something like that he said. I was chilled and giddy when I read his words on the subject. In short, amnesia, the forgetting of the past and the present to bring me closer to one and remove me more from the other, has been my constant state for emotions my whole life. I can remember thinking that way back to my earliest memories. Not sure why, I've often mentioned I was brought home from the hospital the same day the family got its first TV, which had only started broadcasting in Winnipeg 2 years before my birth. Reception was all rabbit ears and very snowy. Together we, the TV and I, learned to communicate with each other. And there were only two channels. But on some mornings, before the Winnipeg channels went on the air, I could see distant snowy transmissions from North Dakota or Minnesota come and go in blizzards of evanescent images, the sound roaring up into an unstable clarity for a few seconds, sometimes a few minutes even, before being suddenly yanked from me, as suddenly as waking from a dream, or as sudden as a death. The experience of watching TV was every bit as dream-addled, every bit as intoxicating as the amnesias in which I accepted myself as immersed. These broadcast interventions alloyed themselves to the melodramas of the soaps, sitcoms and night-time dramas I watched obsessively, and like the leopards in Kafka's famous parable, the leopards that interrupted a sacred ceremony so often they were finally just incorporated into the ceremony, these broadcast interruptions, and my memory interruptions, just became an accepted part of every TV story and my reactions to it. I feel lucky, I got an enriched version of all the programming that probably just bored everyone else. So when as an adult I started to watch noir – and I think it was film writer Lee Server who once called amnesia noir's version of the common cold, I had no trouble as seeing – I didn't even need to "interpret it" – amnesia as the natural state of mind for these post-war PTSD protagonists. The old trope gave me a swift understanding of these doomed chumps. In "women's pictures" I understood better than the average normal kid the tortures and sublimities of Joan Crawford or Ronald Coleman when forgetfulness descended on them. When it came time to make my own movies I turned to trusty old amnesia to help me figure out the human condition. In my earliest most primitive days as screenwriter and director I knew I could never create rich characters, more like the types Buñuel used in *Un Chien andalou* and *L'Age d'Or*, but if I spritzed everyone with amnesia I felt I could give them something like the real human condition, cheaply and quickly. Little did I realize I was giving them my own human condition, which is sold only in novelty shops, not the condition Renoir or Flaubert peddled in their work. Anyway, I think it's especially cinematic because one is already almost completely forgetting the real world when settling into seats inside a dark movie theatre, or in front of a TV screen.

DS

*Like the Brothers Quay you have often cited the novels of Rob-
ert Walser and the stories of Bruno Schulz as an influence,
your films are very different but often speak to comparable
concepts. Is there any further literary common ground between
you? Is it interesting to see how differently your films seem to
digest and communicate these influences? Arguably this link
(with the Quays) could be interesting in light of considering the
darker or 'horror-inflected' elements in your films...*

GM

Yes I adore Walser, and I had been reading his butler
fiction – *Tobold* and *Jakob von Gunten*, just as we were writing
the script for *Careful* (1992). Walser is so gentle, so delicate, so
crazy, it seemed butlering was the perfect profession for *Careful*
because butlers had to be careful always, and quiet, and gentle
and small and almost non-existent, a quiet existence of near zero
presence. The voice of Walser got into my head and I thought I
could profit from such a possession, so I borrowed his tone a lot.
Bruno Schulz gets the way I think. I can't think like him, but he
knows how I go about the process of feeling something and then
reporting that feeling to myself. He does that reporting for me
because I'm no good at it, and since I discovered him I don't need
to worry about the job of feeling. I just read him. That sounds
glib, I know, but it sounds honest to me because I've never fallen
so hard nor so fast for a writer's voice and methods as when I
first encountered Schulz. So powerful was the effect that I am now
misremembering my first encounter with Schulz as contempora-
neous with my earliest childhood memory, and I know that can't
be true.

DS

*Ever since the muffled soundscapes of Archangel (1990); the
discovery of your brother Cameron's old radio recordings; flitting
between stations and distant crackle; and the superb ambient
soundtracks of Jason Staczek – the passage between coherent
and incoherent, whether in memory, vision or sound, seems to*

haunt your films. With the online nature of **Séances** *does this have further implications? You seem to evoke a kind of Youtube glitch effect at times, one that suggests decay as not only the territory of celluloid, or a cinematic past, but continuing into digital possibility.*

GM

I love digital. I completely understand, after decades of marriage to celluloid emulsions, the loyalty Quentin Tarantino and Paul Thomas Anderson feel to film, to 70mm film at that, but they can afford it. I've always been a man forced by low budgets to work the margins of the film industry, the margins of civilization even, and what I've discovered over here on the margin is there's great freedom in low budgets, fewer people, if any, to consult. And there is even greater freedom in the so-called "poor image." Through their lower resolutions lower gauge films like 16mm and super8 conceal as much as they reveal, they can turn glaringly jerry-built worlds into enchanted worlds, just by blurring and graining up the sets and costumes. We're in the middle of a great digital explosion now where the "poor image" is precious to us all. Unstable and murky cell phone images of tragedies have moved a nation to action, no one seems to care if these clips streaming down to us through twitter have high resolution or not. Now everyone is a potential Zapruder, or Arbus, and the textures of digital images are precious to us, they are no longer undesirable simply for reasons of low resolution. There is sublime beauty in all resolutions, and not just for news stories or evidence in a case, but for narrative effects as well. I've been waiting a long time for this moment in film history. This moment in history is nightmarish, but this moment in film history is euphoria inducing. Never have I seen so much potential in moviemaking – thanks to digital. Hybrid genres are proliferating, docufantasias, docudramas, the cine-essay, the essayistic fiction film, every possible permutation, all thanks to the democratization of cameras. I love what digital has done for me, for the work Evan and I made. He was able to massage each of our adapted lost films into its own world of palette and texture. *The Forbidden Room* is a bit like an archaeological dig because with every narrative layer comes a different kind of emulsive loam, a new narrative stratum. One is forced to acknowledge the medium from which the film is fashioned. And I, who have always been inspired most by fairy tales and bedtime stories, love it when the viewer is simultaneously inside a story and aware of its telling. During a bedtime story I was always aware of my grandmother, my sleepytime raconteur. Drowsily I judged her, felt her weight pressing against my legs, compared this night's telling with last week's account of the same story. I listened to her voice and through half-shut eyes beheld her comforting features, but I was also totally inside the story too. I was aware of the medium from which the magic came – my grandmother. I always vowed with my movies I would show viewers the grandmother! The proliferation of artefacts in low budget digital filmmaking allows me to show a grandmother resplendent in raiment's of a glorious poverty, the kind made famous by Mike & George Kuchar, Jack Smith, James Bidgood and John Waters. There is so much heart-breaking beauty to be produced in these little, almost secret studios of the heart. Digital gave me the freedom to spend my money on things other than film processing, and gave me instant feedback on performances. It also gave me images so hideous, on account of my lack of experience with the medium, that we were forced to extreme film decasia to make the images interesting to the eye. But I am thrilled to report that for every tribute to film abrasion we put in the final product, there are as many digital artefacts too. We're just showing the grandmother again! Finally, after being dead since 1970, my grandmother has gone digital!

DS

Returning to the theme of films interacting with poetry – are there any contemporary poets whose work you enjoy? I remember you mentioning Jeremy Dobbs' **Crabwise to the Hounds***, which was a collection I also really loved. What have you been reading recently?*

GM

I should have read these years ago but I am now in the midst of Mary Shelley's Frankenstein and -- hey, Silverblatt! -- Flann O'Brien's *The Dalkey Archive*. So great! I just finished Beckford's *Vathek*, which my filmmaking partner Evan Johnson urged me to read by describing it, way better than I could, as "proto Gabriele D'Annunzio, proto-Huysmans, proto-Flaubert-of-Salammbo, occasionally Rousselian, etched in ultra-precise prose with an enormous vocabulary, but told in a kind of high irony like Mann's *The Holy Sinner*." Now as far as styles go, that's my idea of a collage!

[2015]

JOHN ASHBERY

'... Movies show us ourselves as we had not yet learned to recognize us—something in the nature of daily being or happening that quickly gets folded over into ancient history like yesterday's newspaper'

Ashbery, 'The System' (*Three Poems*, 1972)

The American poet John Ashbery has accumulated a vast and unique body of work: with over twenty volumes of poetry; several plays; a collaborative novel (*A Nest of Ninnies*, written with James Schuyler); collected prose and art criticism; two collections of French translations (in addition to translating Rimbaud's *Illuminations*, Pierre Reveredy's *Haunted House*, much of Giorgio de Chirico's *Hebdomeros* and Pierre Martory's *The Landscapist*); and, most recently, re-imagining a 'lost film' screenplay for Canadian director Guy Maddin. Widely translated, influential and bedecked with almost every award (including a Pulitzer and, more recently, the National Medal of Arts awarded by Barack Obama in 2011), Ashbery's poetry continues to beguile, enchant and confuse with its amorphous ventriloquism of American life.

In the spring of 2009, the Harvard Film Archive organised 'John Ashbery at the Movies', a series of films curated in celebration of his passion for cinema. This included filmmakers who have acknowledged Ashbery as an influence (Abigail Child, Nathaniel Dorsky, Phil Solomon) and films chosen by Ashbery himself. In addition to the active role of film in his poetry, one of the other (many) reasons that this programme came into being was Ashbery's illuminating prose on cinema. His essays, on Jacques Rivette, the phenomenon of Louis Feuillade's *Fantômas*, Val Lewton's *The Seventh Victim*, and Edgar G Ulmer's *Detour*, are all insightful, clearly wrought and downright infectious in their palpable enthusiasm. This conversational impulse between mediums can be traced back to early collaborations with the filmmaker and photographer Rudy Burckhardt, to the close friendship with Frank O'Hara (who in turn often collaborated with filmmaker Alfred Leslie), the invigorating artistic circles gathering around the Tibor de Nagy gallery in 1950s and 60s New York, and, in Ashbery's formative and frequent cinema trips during his time living in Paris.

In Ashbery's poetry the influence of cinema emerges in the experiential shifts of attention that a reading of his poems can induce, as opposed to simply existing referentially or in blatant ekphrasis. For instance, the syntactic disjunction of *The Tennis Court Oath* (Ashbery's boldly experimental second collection, 1962) has been discussed by critic Daniel Kane as a poetic equivalence of the editing techniques of surrealist film. The productive instability of both 'surrealism' and 'film', as concepts and experiences, generates a mobile ambiguity that Ashbery's poetry has long embraced. Rather than simply referring to film, it is instead in the ability of his poems to enact and inspire experiences that, moving between understanding and its sensation or a moment and its expression, poetry and cinema can both be brought into permeable awareness. The crossing of artistic boundaries and contexts, gleefully tickled or blurred, is also clearly at work in Ashbery's interest in collage – which is where this discussion begins…

DS

Do you feel your engagement with visual collages (having now had four exhibitions to date) has changed at all since the summers spent with Joe Brainard, and even earlier experiments throughout college?

JA

I suppose my engagement with collages has expanded now that I am able to show them at a gallery. I've been working on them quite a bit this summer and hoping there will be another show.

DS

Could you possibly say a bit about the collaged play, **The Inn of the Guardian Angel** *(collaged from New York Times obituaries and Hollywood fanzines) that you apparently lent to Guy Maddin during his Seances project?*

JA

He and I were fans of each other's work before we ever met and conversed. His recent *Seances* is beautiful, and of course I love *Archangel, My Winnipeg* and *The Saddest Music in the World*, one of my all-time movie favorites. Yes, *The Inn of the Guardian Angel* is an abandoned project. The title taken from a children's book by the 19th century French (or Russian) children's author Contesse de Ségur. I abandoned it and sent it to Guy telling him he could "strip mine" it for his next movie. I don't think I wrote anything but the "How to Take a Bath" section in his last film. The actor in that film [Louis Negin] who tells an off-color joke (one that I heard in grade school many a year ago) is a sort-of objet trouvé of Guy's, whom he, Guy, has used in a bunch of films.

DS

Let's talk more about film ...

JA

I've always been a fan of movies, and, even more than that, I think the idea of them has somehow informed my work. Do you know my poem 'The Lonedale Operator' in my book *A Wave*? I realized one day that nobody had ever written a poem on the all-important subject of the first movie they ever saw, so I proceeded to do so. It sort of wobbles away from that subject towards the end as my poems tend to do!

DS

Could you say a bit about 'John Ashbery at the Movies', the programme of films coordinated by Haden Guest and Scott Macdonald at the Harvard Film Archive?

JA

First off, 'John Ashbery at the Movies' was quite interesting to me, as I had forgotten some of the films and not seen others. The younger filmmakers who were apparently influenced by me were particularly appealing, notably Abigail Child, who is famous but whom I didn't know before then, and I especially liked Phil Solomon's film *The Exquisite Hour*. Also the Busby Berkeley and Daffy Duck films were just as I remembered them. I was a little disappointed in a French film called *Adieu Léonard*, which I had seen many years ago in Paris and remembered as a bizarre and delightful comedy. It was just OK. It was made during the Occupation and has some of the creepy brilliance of many of the films of that time. (One I particularly recommend is Called *Douce* by Claude Autant-Lara, a 19th Century romantic tear-jerker that features the famous character actress Marguerite Moréno as an obnoxious old rich lady).

DS

I once read somewhere that you recommended **The Psychotronic Encyclopedia of Film** *(Michael Weldon), do you still have this? I have a copy (as a result of that recommendation), it's an absolute treasure-trove of trash…in all the best ways. I love it. Do you have any other books about or on film that have been important to you?*

JA

I hope I do still have a copy of *The Psychotronic Encyclopedia of Film*, though I haven't seen it around lately. I can't think of other books on film that have been important, except for the Hallowell guides and Leonard Maltin's guides for catching films on TV. That book was useful when I wrote a poem, "They Knew What They Wanted," where every line was a movie title that began with "they."

DS

Are there any other poets that share your particular taste in movies? Or poets whose work flirts with film in ways that interest you?

JA

Frank O'Hara and I both were on the same wavelength with regard to movies. Also John Yau has written an essay on going to the movies with me, which I haven't read in a long time, but is quite probably very informative. Robert Polito writes interestingly about film in his poetry.

DS

Two of your favourite films, **On Approval** *(1944) and* **Dead of Night** *(1945), showcase the charms of British actress "Googie" Withers (Georgette Lizette Withers)...*

JA

By coincidence I saw *On Approval* and *Dead of Night* just a few weeks ago on TV. The marvelous channel Turner Classic Movies had a sort of mini Googie festival, which also included *It Always Rains On Sunday*, which as its title would suggest is rather dreary. I first saw *Dead of Night* sometime in the late forties, at a time when I used to view movies serially. I probably saw it around 20 times along with such other faves as René Clair's *Le Million* and Clive Brook's *On Approval*, maybe my all-time favorite. Bea Lillie was magnificent as the wealthy spinster Maria Wislack and Googie Withers perhaps even greater as the nice person in the movie. It's funny about *Dead of Night*. When I first saw it in Boston in the 40s the golf links sequence wasn't shown, I had to wait until my 16th or 17th viewing in order to see it. Googie again gives her all, especially when she is about to be strangled by her husband and looks in the antique mirror to discover a strange interior and manages to break the mirror just before her husband, whose name momentarily eludes me, almost does her in. I forgot to mention Cocteau's *Orphée*, which was also part of my compulsive cinema-going.

DS

Having written with affection on Val Lewton's films (produced for RKO pictures), specifically **The Seventh Victim** *(1943), I was wondering if films from the 40s seem to retain a certain resonance or significance for you, and if so, why?*

JA

I suppose 40s films have a certain "resonance or significance" for me, perhaps because that was the period of my adolescence when I was starting to go out and see things on my own and draw my own conclusions about them. *The Seventh Victim* is one of my all-time favorite movies, not just for its dark and forbidding atmosphere but for the sort of endearing clunky-ness it was made with. The totally obscure actress Jean Brooks exerts a mysterious magnetism.

There seems to be a certain way of appreciating a film that relates a sense of Surrealism to interpretive reception and not the film's design, often a more potent experience than watching any self-declared 'Surrealist' film. In prioritising our own attentions as viewers, as opposed to a film's original intentionality, certain details become lyrical: you describe the portrayal of New York in The Seventh Victim in this way, and the background décor and genius loci of Feuillade's Fantômas films. Can you think of any other films that have struck you in this way...arguably all film, in the right moment or frame of mind!?

JA

Offhand, a film I saw last night for the first time, again on TCM, a 1946 film noir titled *The Dark Corner,* starring Mark Stevens, Lucille Ball (in her pre-Lucy days--she was quite good in a straight role) as well as reliable villains Clifton Webb and Kurt Kreuger. Actually, the boundary between surrealist films and just any films is sort of undefinable. That's what draws us to movies I guess. I'll try to remember some partially surreal films for you. There is a very good short one called *La Perle*, written by the surrealist poet Georges Hugnet. More recently there are of course the wonderful films of Jacques Rivette, of which I am particularly fond, especially *Out One/Spectre* and *Céline and Julie Go Boating.* And of course Guy Maddin, whose surrealism is closely linked to his extreme nostalgia for old films.

DS

In a 2002 interview with Mark Ford, you made a very interesting observation in which you related the 'disintegration' of Language poetry to that of Surrealism – suggesting 'there's a certain hard kernel that can stand the pressure for only so long, and then it starts to decay, giving off beneficial fumes.' Are there any poets who particularly stand out for you, in their reaction to, or incorporation of, this fruitful 'disintegration' of Surrealism?

I've always felt that most surrealist poetry is disappointing when compared to the vague feelings that the word surrealism conjures up, even in daily, TV man-on-the-street interviews— "Hurricane Sandy was really surreal." This admittedly inchoate concept is curiously more useful than the glacial surfaces of Breton and Éluard. I do love the poetry of Jacob and Reverdy, but they weren't "officially" surrealists, as far as I know. Perhaps they would be "poets who particularly stand out in their reaction to, or incorporation with this fruitful disintegration," though they seem much less decadent than that would imply.

'*to communicate only through this celluloid vehicle that has immortalized and given a definitive shape to our formless gestures; we can live as though we had caught up with time and avoid the sickness of the present, a shapeless blur as meaningless as a carelessly exposed roll of film.*'

Ashbery, 'The System' (*Three Poems*, 1972)

[This interview draws from correspondence between 2013-2016]

SO MAYER

So Mayer has six collections of poetry, several chapbooks and has appeared in and edited numerous anthologies, in addition to which they are consistently writing some of the best film criticism around. In 2009, Mayer's *The Cinema of Sally Potter: A Politics of Love* provided one of the first scholarly accounts of Potter's unique and challenging work in film. More recently in 2015, *Political Animals: The New Feminist Cinema* arrived, offering a much overdue and masterful exploration of what has come to constitute the active counter tradition of feminist cinema and its innovation. From out of the dialogues between feminist thinking, the exclusionary and insidious politics of representation, and the poetics of film that in turn question film in and as poetry, Mayer's own collections of poetry have continued to pierce and problematize

Their poems are drawn to tensions between the corporeal and the conceptual, between the body and its language; these are spaces – at once vulnerable and violent – that Mayer's poetry returns to with sharp intelligence. On top of which, the poems are often shot through with dark wit or mischievous humour. Able to communicate nuanced readings of the body and its experiences, their poetry manages to successfully challenge and express the intellect without ever renouncing physicality and its embodied attentions...or perhaps, more perceptively, refuses any such polarity. This is then added to Mayer's scholarly fluency in film, creating a body (and it is emphatically *a body*) of poetry that examines text and screen in the politics of our own personal encounters.

DS

In a recent interview, concerning the intersections between film and poetry, you suggested that there is

SM

a resistance to connections between poetry and cinema in the UK in anything other than an almost-music video form, but the feminists in each community share so many concerns

**about the limits of conventional language and the excitement
of experiment that I want to be a mediator, rather than focus
on one form.**

*I recognize the 'almost-music video' approach, so often
a painful exercise in literalism, where metaphors are visualized
and a self-consciously 'poetic' aesthetic is invoked as opposed
to an active poetics. However, as you detail in your essay
'Cinema mon Amour: How British Poetry Fell in Love with Film',
there are poets incorporating cinema in ways that clearly resist
this narrative. Are there any contemporary British poets and
filmmakers you feel are particularly engaged in this dialogue? If
so, what is it that interests you about them?*

SM

With the increase in artist-filmmakers producing feature
-length films, there has been an incredible flowering of
awareness about the possibilities of bringing film and
poetry together: John Akomfrah's *The Nine Muses* and *The Stuart
Hall Project* and Sarah Turner's *Public House* stand out for me.
Interestingly, in both *The Stuart Hall Project* and *Public House*,
William Blake's poetics are to the fore. The revival of interest
in Blake as a visual poet or poet-artist, as someone for whom
verbal and visual forms were inextricable, is incredibly important
to both film and poetry cultures in the UK. Both Akomfrah and
Turner are committed to a liberatory politics similar to Blake's,
one that is both grassroots and ecstatic.

That's what interests me in hybrid work: when poetry explores
and draws on cinema's collective and active spectatorship; and
when film engages poetry's tradition of apostrophe and of formal
innovation. There's a temptation for each form to mimic or be
drawn to the most mainstream and obvious iteration of the other;
but when, for example, Redell Olsen recuts early documentary
footage of commercial lacemakers and writes in response to both
the movement of the lacemakers' bodies and the movement across
the cuts in the film (in *Film Poems*), that is a thrilling expansion of
the possibilities of both forms, and one that also draws attention
to the forgotten, obscured and under-seen.

I'm hoping that the incredible box set, curated by Sarah Neely, of the work of Margaret Tait will follow up on the amazing work done by Peter Todd in drawing attention to Tait's utterly unique body of work – and its connections to many threads in post-war British arts. While Tait died in 1999, the persistence, revival and recovery of her work makes it very much of the present – not least that the revival belongs both to work by the Scottish poetry community and the British film community.

DS

How significant do you believe the London Filmmakers Co-op was (and perhaps is, in its influence) in considering the experimentation between British poetry and film? As 'Cinema mon Amour' did not look to address this question, I was interested in whether this was a conscious choice made in resistance to certain patriarchal histories of the avant-garde?

SM

As *From Reel to Real: Women, Feminism and the London Film-Makers' Co-operative* showed (this past weekend at Tate Modern), it is indeed the histories, and not the history, that is patriarchal. Women were deeply involved in the Co-op, starting in the 1970s with Gill Eatherley, Annabel Nicolson and Sally Potter (whose later feature-length works I do discuss in the essay), as well as Lis Rhodes, Tina Keane, Jayne Parker, Nina Danino, Tania and Alia Syed, Sandra Lahire, Sarah Pucill, Sarah Turner (whose new feature *Public House* I mention above), Ruth Novaczek, Cordelia Swann, Vanda Carter and more. Many of these women were also involved with Four Corners, and/or with the distribution co-ops Circles and Cinema of Women. But they have been written out of histories of British artists' film and video, absolutely.

The essay was written for a history of British and Irish poetry, so my focus was on the literature and orature of poetry, as it responded to film and was responded to in film, rather than on the complex discussion of film's own poetics and the definition of a filmpoem (or poemfilm). The word 'poetic' is used extremely loosely to refer to any film that does not subscribe to mainstream aesthetics (and thus uses 'poetic' to mean some insidious, reductively Romantic notion somewhere between non-linear, pastoral, lyric, imagistic, etc.) In more rigorous ways, avant-garde filmmakers have sought to loosen the strictures of mainstream film 'grammar' (particularly influenced by film semiotics), for example through the structuralism that was the LFMC's initial credo.

There is definitely more research and writing to be done on parallel trends in experimental poetry and experimental film, but my essay focused on where the two came together in a single text – and I tried to focus on film work that would be readily available to readers approaching the question of film and poetry from the poetry side. I wish I'd had the opportunity to talk, for example, about Lahire's 16mm black and white film 'Lady Lazarus' an invocation and summoning of Plath and her poetry.

DS

In writing for **Sight & Sound***, you have consistently sought to combat what you have called the 'myth of scarcity' in discussing female filmmakers. You have also appeared in the Shearsman poetry anthology* **Infinite Difference: Other Poetries by UK Women***, a book that dispels this 'myth of scarcity' in a poetic context. How do you feel your experience of film and poetry communities compare in supporting under-represented identities?*

SM

I'm taking the phrase the 'myth of scarcity' from an article by the poet Jill McDonagh that appeared on VIDA, titled 'Believing in Plenty.' The comment you quote in your first question could equally refer to the way in which feminist artists are brought together across the boundaries between media and practices by this drive toward believing in plenty. Feminist-oriented experimental poetry spaces such as POLYply were also multimedia, screening films by American poet-filmmaker Abigail Child (and one of the leading theorists of feminist filmpoetics), for example.

There's no homogenous "film" or "poetry" community: there are different actions and movements at different times in each community, and I'm most interested in where they cross over, or where feminist community formations trump those around an artform or genre. I grew up in zine culture, where verbal, visual and sonic arts moved in alignment and hybridised with each other, and I see that returning in contemporary projects such as gal-dem.

DS

Aside from swiftly buying your new book **Political Animals: The New Feminist Cinema***, what advice would you give to people looking to read or see more work that explores experimentation alongside, or inseparable from, contemporary feminism? Could you maybe explain a bit about the role of Club Des Femmes?*

SM

Club des Femmes is a queer feminist film curation collective based in London, founded in 2007 by Selina Robertson and Sarah Wood, who are both programmers and filmmakers. It emerged from their passion for feminist experimental cinema (and the collective and discursive ways in which it was made), and their frustration at a lack of spaces in which it could be screened in context and conversation. Over nearly a decade, Club des Femmes has been part of a huge shift towards communitarian curation (partially enabled by digital projection) with an emphasis on foregrounding alternative and experimental cinema within event-based programming. There are new queer film festivals such as FRINGE! (London), SQIFF and GLITCH! (both Glasgow), as well as spaces like Liverpool Small Cinema, which is curated by a collective including Elsewhere Cinema, which programmed *58%*, foregrounding films by women, trans and non-binary filmmakers. LUX and Cinenova, which distribute experimental and feminist films respectively, have just moved to a new venue with a screening space. So I think this is an incredibly exciting moment for people to access films outside the mainstream.

In addition, many intersectional feminist collectives such as gal-dem screen films as part of their events and online presence; video diaries, documentaries, music videos, animation, experimental shorts – these are a core part of the language of fourth-wave feminism, and they are often channelling the influence of all kinds of historical feminist experimentation. If you watched Beyoncé's *Lemonade*, you watched a film influenced by the LA Rebellion cinema of Julie Dash, and you can see the restoration of her film *Daughters of the Dust* at the London Film Festival (and hopefully touring thereafter) this October. You can also see the restoration of Lizzie Borden's legendary feminist science fiction film *Born in Flames* at the same festival, which was one of Club des Femmes' very first screenings. The words 'experimental' and 'feminist' sound challenging, but this is work that has permeated our culture.

DS

I think you have mentioned 'poethics' in an interview I read somewhere...I was wondering – given your contribution to **Catechism: Poems for Pussy Riot** *and your continued engagement with active voices of feminism, queer poetics and issues of misrepresentation (across cinema and poetry) – what your views on poetry as activism are?*

SM

Poethics is feminist poet and scholar Joan Retallack's word; she talks about the 'poethical wager' in her 2003 book of the same name. Ethics – and activism – begin in language for me, and hence there is no poetry (or communication) that is not activism. Take citational practices, for example: whose work you foreground, how and where you name them, what gets foot noted and what doesn't, whose work you reference/foreground/ epigraph/pastiche and how. These are political acts. Of course, they're not the only political or ethical acts, but too often we assume a capital-P Political, both as part of a spectrum of signifi- cance with Political Poetry (generally satire or war poetry) at the top; and as part of a binary, as if there were Political Poetry and all other work were apolitical (by design). If language is political and ethical, then you can choose to ignore that, but then your work inscribes dominant politics as a matter of course.

So my activism begins at the level of the word. But I am also an avowedly activist writer, although that means different things at different times – collective editing work, collaborative writing work (with Sarah Crewe), bringing poetry into alternative spaces (like experimental feminist film screenings), teaching radical histories of poetry, reviewing and advocating for other activist writers and publications, and being activist within my own creative practice.

DS

In **Her Various Scalpels** *(Shearsman, 2009) you begin with a sequence entitled 'star poems', each is 'after' a film (Lynne Stopkewich's* **Kissed***, Michael Winterbottom's* **9 songs***, Anthony Minghella's* **The English Patient***, Sally Potter's* **The Gold Diggers***, Rebecca Miller's* **The Ballad of Jack and Rose***, Sofia Coppola's* **The Virgin Suicides***, and Lucrecia Martel's* **La Niña Santa***). Though this initially seems like an explicit dialogue, the poems are inventively skewed. The mentioned films seem to become tonal indicators for how to enter the poetic space, rather than a more familiar ekphrastic response of about-ness... what was it that drew you to these particular films? They would make for a fascinating programme of screenings!*

SM

I wrote those poems over a decade ago, so I'm reconstructing from memory. *The Gold Diggers* was out of circulation for a very long time – from its initial release in 1983 until its DVD release in 2009. I was lucky enough to see it on video in 2005, when I was first researching my book on Sally Potter, and it made a very deep impression on me. I think that was the kernel of the series, which posed a question (as the film does) about the female performer as star – literally, as a light source. That visual metaphor is present in *Kissed*, where it refers to a spiritual experience of female sexuality, and in *The Virgin Suicides*, where the remembered Lisbon sisters appear to emit light. These female performers draw attention to themselves, and thus to the film as film, and to our responses to watching film – they are asterisks, textual markers as well as astronomical bodies.

I'm not a big fan of about-ness, in the sense of a narrative centred on a character or theme. What interests me about the ekphrastic is the formal challenge of moving image language from one medium to another – but even more than that, the potential for disruption. In epic poetry, ekphrastes are interruptions: a pause in a dramatic scene to look closely at a

57

visual detail that might present a counter-narrative, prophetic insight or thematic parallel, but is also often riotously sensual and attentive to the skill of the visual artist (and thus offers parallels for the poet's skill). It's reflexive, hybrid and a form of poetics: not just description. Or rather, description is never just description, it's a theory of optics, narratology, form, relation, etc.

Each of the poems begins by looking at the films' 'about-ness' (*9 Songs* is about a straight couple having sex and listening to bands) and then asks what else there is to a film, other than a plot summary – the films I chose have a strong sense of their own reflexive use of the medium, their critique of about-ness. I love the oblique use of sound in *La Niña Santa*, for example, and the chaptering of *9 Songs* which is really quite stringent and structuralist. All of them are (now I think about it) also films about loss, but none of them are elegiac (or in *The Virgin Suicides*, the masculinist elegiac is somewhat satirised); instead, they vividly summon what has been lost (which is almost always female or feminine) into presence; often, as in *The English Patient*, that summoning exceeds the frame that is meant to hold it – and that excess, I guess, became what fed the poems.

DS

I find the eroticism that runs throughout many of your poems a really interesting element – one that is able to prickle with wit, but also playfully enjoy itself. Do you ever find that the 'playful' – as a dynamic that is restless/mobile/mutable – can speak to queerness as well as maybe a kind of Surrealism? Could eroticism be a space in poetry and film for gender and sexual fluidity to explore, and be explored by, kinds of Surrealism?

SM

There's a lot of terms imbricating each other here: eroticism, playfulness, queerness, Surrealism. I think they all have historied relations to one another that are complex and worth drawing out: for example, Breton's dismissal of Cocteau from the Surrealist movement because of his sexuality. Rosalind Krauss' writing on Surrealism has been very influential on my critical thinking, as have the scholars of women Surrealists. The big *Angels of Anarchy* show at Manchester Art Gallery in 2009, which I loved, made it clear that many women (and many queer women) operated under the banner of Surrealism, often making the most inventive and persuasive work by putting gender and sexual fluidity and fantasy at the centre, like Eileen Agar or Dora Maar or Meret Oppenheimer or Frida Kahlo (although she disclaimed identification with Surrealism). So I think that those possibilities have already been realised, but have been written out of the standard histories and gallery accounts.

Angela Carter and Kathy Acker were hugely influential writers that I discovered as a teenager, and both of them were unabashed in their erotic play with literary form. And there are similar feminist erotics of form in the work of Lizzie Borden, Cheryl Dunye, Sandra Lahire, Chantal Akerman, Ulrike Ottinger, Hito Steyerl, Tejal Shah… the list goes on.

DS

I LOVE your collection (O) (Arc, 2009), the poem 'Silence, Singing' was, for me, a particularly stunning beast! As quite a long poem, taking its form in fragments of prose, it plays with the essay form and though your collection mentions both Susan Howe and Anne Carson, I was wondering whether essay-films may also have had an influence on its style and rhythms?

SM

Absolutely. But both Howe and Carson have written about film: Carson particularly about Antonioni (and particularly his lesser-known documentary work, in her essay 'Foam', in *Decreation*), and Howe about Marker, in *Sorting Facts, or Nineteen Ways of Looking at Marker* (who was a book designer as well as a filmmaker…). So the 21st century feminist poetic essay is already infused with the essay-film – and vice versa. One of the first essay-films is Forough Farrokhzad's *Khaneh sia ast* ('The House is Black'), from 1962 – Farrokhzad was a poet as well as a filmmaker, and a truly revolutionary artist.

'Silence, Singing' is actually one of the least consciously cinematically-inflected pieces of writing I've done, although I think the fragmentary form, and the movement between thoughts, is definitely shaped by an immersion in the work of filmmakers such as Sarah Turner, Sarah Wood, John Akomfrah, etc. There's only one directly filmically imagistic moment in it, and it's quite hidden: when I'm overlaying Iphigenia and Bathsheba standing at the military camp, my internal visualisation was shaped by Michael Cacoyannis' film *Iphigenia*.

DS

The last poem in that collection, a signature poem no less ('The Mayer') has some of the most dizzyingly wonderful collisions: 'Albus Einstein's particles and Gertrude / Stein's participles' being a particular favourite! Film and poetry can play with time in varying ways – are there any particular poets or filmmakers that for you offer exciting new ways to experience or understand time? Apologies – I know the list could be endless... but it just seemed like the ending of (O) was significantly drawn into this question, looking into 'this ever-present. (O) dazzle of mayhappening'.

SM

It's an answering (or bracketing) signature poem: the opening poem is called Sophia (which was my given name, although I changed it by usage when I was five). So it's definitely about enfolding and cyclicity, as the section titles of the book suggest (I Do, I Undo, I Redo). It's a stand against time's arrow and the insistent eschatological linearity of colonial heteropatriarchy. We need to think about this aspect of time, it's critical – and political. It's a theory of history as much as anything.

I love Agnès Varda walking back... back... back... surrounded by mirrors in *The Beaches of Agnès* (and her precise jokes with time in *Cléo de 5 à 7*). The spirals of time, repetition, and remembering in Sally Potter's *The Gold Diggers*. The incremental seriality of Inger Christensen's *It* (translated by Susannah Nied). *Always Coming Home* and 'A Fisherman of the Inland Sea' by Ursula K. Le Guin. Maya Deren's handling of space-as-time in 'Meshes of the Afternoon' and 'At Land'. Allison Adele Hedge Coke's unwriting of colonial time and reinscription of indigenous (including non-human) temporalities in *Blood Run*. *Blood Run* and *It* are both book-length sequences that offer cosmogonies and cosmic time, although their sequentiality is quite differently structured. Ambitious without being over bearing, generous yet rigorous: I think the feminist long poem/book-length sequence, as it works through and deconstructs both the realist novelistic narrative and the militaristic nationalist epic (going back to Howe and Carson from the previous question, but also Bhanu Kapil, Claudia Rankine, Karthika Nair, Liz Howard, Lucas de Lima) is where the unwriting of time is at in contemporary poetry.

DS

Are there particular poets or filmmakers that you return to for inspiration? What films or books kick-start the imagination or restore your faith in all things cine/poetic?

SM

See above! What I like about working as a curator and critic and teacher and editor, as well as an artist, is getting to cross back through works or artists I've previously encountered, but from a different perspective, or framing them differently, or with a different audience. Pairing Rankine's *Citizen: An American Lyric* with Marker's *Sans Soleil* for a class this year, for example, to think about what bell hooks calls 'black looks.' Or screening Abigail Child's film about Mary Shelley, *A Shape of Error*, with readings by Sophie Robinson and Isabel Waidner. It's about activating the re-readings or re-encounters as much as anything.

For private sustenance, I do return frequently to Le Guin's *The Dispossessed*, to Charlotte Brontë's *Villette*, to Audre Lorde's *Sister Outsider*, Chrystos' *In Her I Am*: books I encountered in my late teens and early 20s, when I was working things out. (And Tori Amos lyrics.) I'm also always quoting Judith Butler's *Precarious Life* (it's the epigraph to (O)).

After writing Political Animals, which discusses over 500 films, my relationship to cinema has changed somewhat – there's a certain fatigue, particularly with mainstream cinema. Probably the film I've rewatched most from the films I talk about there is *Belle* (Amma Asante), but it was also a cue to revisit films I'd seen at festivals and half-remembered like *The Time We Killed* by Jennifer Reeves. Festivals and curated programmes are where I do a lot of my viewing now: it's quite social, and as much about context as content. That said, I am very excited to see the restorations of *Born in Flames* and *Daughters of the Dust*, and the first features by Margaret Salmon and Hope Dickson Leach, and Desperate Optimists' *Further Beyond*, at the LFF. I've fallen in love with the work of American short filmmaker Jennifer Reeder over the last year, and Thai filmmaker Anocha Suwichakornpong.

In poetry, what excites me here and now is the relation of new writing to editorial and curatorial projects: for the UK alone, Dorothy Lehane and Litmus, Sarah Crewe and aglimpseof, Andrea Brady and Archive of the Now, Theo Chiotis and Futures, Eleanor Perry, Juha Virtanen and Datableed. Nisha Ramayya, Eley Williams, Prudence Chamberlain and Generative Constraints. Sam Solomon, Joe Luna, Natalia Cecire and The Sussex Poetry Festival. And so many more. The inventive, joyous effervescence of creating alternative spaces for embodied, political poetics.

[2016]

R<small>EDELL</small> O<small>LSEN</small>

It is impossible to discuss the intersections between contemporary poetry and film in Britain without mentioning Redell Olsen. Olsen has continually turned to the extensions and echoes of poetry in the art world in service of broadening and complicating the possibilities of her work. Avant-garde history, feminist theory, modernist poetics, and the temporal and spatial politics of everything therein, all are dissected and redirected in Olsen's traversals across art, text and visuals. Her readings have explored site-specific performance and blurring the parameters of academic and artistic presentation; confusing and pushing form to bear the trace of its dialogues and multiplicity. In addition to her poetry, Olsen has edited the influential *How2* journal that has explored, showcased and archived experimental writing by women for over three decades (since 1983). She is also Professor of Poetry and Poetics at Royal Holloway. What remains so important and inspiring about Olsen's multi-disciplinary poetics is its intelligent and unflinching commitment to the tensions that complicate and constitute moving between forms.

DS

I wanted to begin by asking you about your experimentation with narrative in 'Corrupted by Showgirls' (in Secure Portable Space, Reality Street Editions, 2004). You seem to transpose filmic jump-cuts into syntax, questioning both language and film in the collapsing and condensing of narrative – or, as Drew Milne phrases it, the poem 're-animates the narrative grammar of noir femininity'. What were the main inspirations behind this? At times, I felt as though Abigail Child's film sequence Is This What You Were Born For (1981-89) was being evoked, especially through the poem's use of genre and its interrogation of gender –was this a point of reference for you?

RO

I think that these are interesting ways of describing what I was doing in this particular sequence of poems...In terms of how they were written some were based on notes taken while writing through various Noir films in real time and others in response to existing critical writing on these films – including synopses. I do indeed admire Abigail Child's films and writing although she wasn't a direct influence at the time -- some years after I wrote 'Corrupted by Showgirls' I wrote an essay about her films. Joan Retallack's 'Memnoir' which I reviewed when it came out – again after the fact of writing my poem - could also be compared to them in terms of related ideas ("Joan Retallack's Memnoir," Poetry Project Newsletter # 201, December/January, 2004-2005)). I was also interested in Cindy Sherman's early 'Untitled Film Stills'. And on a very different tack, Barbara Guest's work was very instructive for its shaping and refracted sense of lines and she has also written some wonderful prose poems that relate very directly to film. Another influence over 'Secure Portable Space' as a whole book is the poet Charles Olson.

DS

Throughout 'Corrupted by Showgirls' you twist language into the cinematographic (via its sense of editing techniques of cuts or montage, in addition to its content) only to veer out and bare its mechanisms –inviting a parallel in the formalist materiality behind the composition of film and of language; no longer simply 'narrative film' or 'poetry' but the materiality of such constructs at work. Do you feel this to be a poetics interacting with legacies of Language poetry, or some of the Structuralist or formalist work in the London Filmmakers' Co-Op?

RO

These are all important reference points for this poem. However, I see this as being work that is primarily influenced and in tension with possibilities of Language writing (which was the subject of the Phd that I was writing at the time - *Scripto-Visualities: Visual Arts and Contemporary Writing by Women*). There is a great quote by Carla Harryman where she says, "I prefer to distribute narrative rather than to deny it…" ("Toy Boats," Poets Journal 6, 1986) that was productively on my mind when I was writing. I am also very interested in the film and live performances of Carolee Schneeman who I know was associated with the London Filmmakers' Co-Op - also the traditions of the Nouveau Roman as it developed in relation to film through writing by Marguerite Duras and Alain Robbe-Grillet.

DS

Did you begin to work in film after writing poetry – or did the two always exist in tandem for you? I feel as though one is always scored through with the other in your work, as though never entirely present as film or poetry in a confined sense. The poetry often acts like a trace left by the, now absent, visual happening or film (like 'Era of Heroes' or the collected works in Film Poems) and therefore the work seems to always play with incomplete-ness? Or what cannot be contained? This is really exciting as it certainly feels closer to the permeable dialogue or 'hybridized form' that many other works purport to exercise... but that, unlike your work, instead become ekphrastic or like short-sighted asides in representation.

RO

That is very astute, thank you. My parents are both painters so I grew up with a strong commitment and understanding of the visual - that was the given that I could move out from and choose to return to. I am deeply indebted to my parents for an understanding of process in the making of work. Various contexts have obviously been important since: I studied English Literature for my first degree at the University of Cambridge and J.H. Prynne supervised my dissertations. I also attended Rod Mengham's lectures that made links between contemporary writing, theory and American poetics. I was interested in the poetry that I read and heard at Cambridge at CCCP events in the early 1990s: a mixture of British, French and American influences. I subsequently studied for a foundation in Art and Design and then a Masters in Fine Art – where I worked mainly with photography, performance and installed texts. Later on I completed an academic PhD at the University of London (with Prof. Robert Hampson)....

This is all a round about way of saying that I work with various forms of text: both image and language and have done for most of my life. The balance changes in relation to the contexts of production, distribution. In terms of the recent film poems that I have made it varies in terms of what comes first. I wrote 'Bucolic Picnic' as one draft and then cut the found footage together and wrote more with the knowledge that it would be performed live in relation to that footage. For 'Sprigs and Spots' I slowed the film down and then had to cut down the text that I had. I was also very concerned with that film poem that it should also make reference and be considered visually in relation to the page of the book itself. So, the text is mediating a sense of its possibility in the space of film and live performance but also the performance of the work on the page – something that conventional script work even of the experimental kind doesn't usually tend to do.

I am actually really interested in the possibilities of ekphrastic writing and have a sequence that I wrote in 2012 called, 'Performances for Paintings' that responded to particular paintings with directions for a parallel performance or action that might actually never be fully realised. Their deliberate 'incompleteness' (somewhere between documentation and score) was in part triggered by a sense of frustration with some of the limitations of a tradition that often seemed to offer very literal 'translations' of paintings - rather than what I wanted to write which were conceptual provocations in dialogue with existing works of art.

DS

Do you think that the notion of 'interdisciplinary' or 'hybridized' forms are often valued more in theory than in practice or execution? I'm thinking here of the discourse surrounding funding bodies and academia in which the 'interdisciplinary' is conceptually worshipped...but its actual existence often seems fairly rare...as though there are polite and accepted forms of 'interdisciplinary' practice that do little else than safely confirm a division between mediums: e.g. here are some poems-about or in response to [insert non-specific art project]...whereby poetry or text is reduced to an ornamental or meditative reflection, as opposed to embodying any active interaction.

RO

Yes that is a problem. I suppose that you have to make the work that you are interested in making and hope that the culture around you likes it enough to want to support its development.

What writers or artists do you think are currently doing interesting work actively crossing between film and poetry?

RO

There are a number of very good recent graduates from the MA in Poetic Practice and subsequent practice based PhD programme at Royal Holloway such as Nisha Ramayya and John Sparrow who are making interesting work that crosses film / performance and the digital. I am also interested in the current film and text work being made by my friend, the artist Gillian Wylde who had a show at the Arnolfini in 2016. The live version of Caroline Bergvall's 'Drift' is an impressive collaboration between her and a musician and artist that involves music, poetry and film.

DS

Could you say a little bit about the context or inspiration behind Punk Faun: A Bar Rock Pastel (Subpress, 2012)? The book's blurb entangles its synopsis with: a commission by Isabelle d'Este; the art book 'THEY CALLED HER STYRENE' by Ed Ruscha; a screening of Matthew Barney's 'Cremastser'; the installations of Max Neuhaus; a mutation of the pastoral, at once mythic and modern; an experience in a karaoke bar; and the 'plight of deer on the roads of Europe and North America... would it be fair to say, that in busy disorientation the book finds its (non-locatable) point of departure, 'in which even the title was against itself'?

RO

These are indeed some of the points of reference and certainly to me very locatable points of departure! I wanted to write a kind of baroque vision (hence the bar rock obviously) through which to think about the contemporary. And yes, everything is in contradiction or against itself: the faun/fawn (a colour, a deer, a gesture of subservience) and the day-glo of punk possibilities set in impossible relation to the Renaissance.

I imagined the whole as a series of texts to be streamed on a wall, partly in reference to Isabella D'Este's 'studiolo' - which is a domestic and secular space for which she commissioned artists to make work on the walls and ceilings of her rooms - and more mundane considerations of public spaces of contemplation such as the arcade, the mall... The book's starting point is a reimagining of this studiolo as book – the poems as possible texts to be installed that make reference to recent art, contemplation, performance, life, gender, power...

DS

In the use of repetition and rhythm, especially in 'variants marked points of' and 'snares for silence in required voice', the poetry seems to find a real mischievous enjoyment through introducing formal codes from the pastoral into a realm of avant-garde instability. Does this element of time, moving between an arcane or outmoded form or work (I'm thinking here too of 'A Newe Booke of Copies'), and a more contemporary poetics, also inform your film work?

RO

That is very interesting, yes – although I don't see these as arcane or outmoded forms but forms that can be called upon, utilised and brought into dialogue with more contemporary rhythms and sounds – hopefully to make new forms of poetic practice that acknowledge their relationship to a variety of forms and existing traditions. The film work often uses found material from different periods also. I suppose in each I am interested in establishing and expanding on connections and threads that might link apparently disparate or at first glance redundant images and ideas.

DS

How does engaging versions of the historical (whatever that might be...!), or destabilising its narrative, influence your practice?

Certainly in *Punk Faun* I was interested in engaging with alternative time frames and multiple possibilities of reference and juxtaposition – often in fluid simultaneity. It is a way of working that certainly has implications for the possible destabilisation of the various histories, source materials or forms that it draws on. Hopefully the work begins to stand in relation to these borrowings rather than become one with them. I hope that in juxtaposition new relationships and possible connections are established that might go some way to returning the found, the historical, the past, the overlooked to a having a direct relevance to the contemporary moment of production not to stand in place of this. I am not interested in the work being nostalgically 'about' any of these sources - they are materials / forms with which to engage in the contemporary.

DS

Who have been important artists for influencing your approach? As your work spans and draws from film, poetry, academia and the visual arts – is there a particular medium, field or figure that ever takes precedence?

RO

It is true my work - as I do, draws on practices from different genres. Allen Fisher's work in all its visual and verbal crossing is exciting to me and I am always excited to encounter new work by writers such as Lisa Robertson, Juliana Spahr, Judith Goldman and Jena Osman. Each of them is making (very different) work with reference points that continually step outside conventional frames and all engage with what I feel is a highly constructive and relevant poetics for the contemporary.

DS

Are you working on any new projects? What is currently interesting you?

I have a bookwork in an exhibition that is currently in London (curated by Susan Johanknecht and Finlay Taylor). The book is called 'Mox Nox' and amongst other things it borrows from mottoes for sundials as a starting point for some of the writing. It uses images from 19th Century sources detailing Arctic exploration. It also involves a different kind of the filmic than the one that we have mostly been discussing here – in the case of this book a film of photosensitive adhesive paper that has been applied to various parts of the page so that it changes colour temporarily in daylight, so in theory the text should alter as you read it. I suppose that is also an important sense of what film is for me – the almost imperceptible and often porous surface between entities, ideas, images, words – different forms of practice.

[2017]

JOHN ADAMS

In his 1985 film, *Intellectual Properties*, John Adams created a work that is at once intimately redolent of its time and eerily prescient to a range of contemporary experiences: of politics and the virtual; advertising and the personal; escalations of capitalism and the value of art beyond, before and because of economic value; time and the desire for narrative as seduced by the media and its narratives of desire; and, of course, that time-honoured and lesser-known artistic pilgrimage of Newcastle to Boston...the transatlantic journey. Originally presented as a 6-monitor installation and later edited as a single one hour film, *Intellectual Properties*, jostles between 16mm footage and video-editing. It uses looped repetition to re-contextualise and manipulate reoccurring motifs, encouraging (or teasing) a sense of possible (and pluralised) narrative and itching between vocabularies of noir, surveillance, travelogue, documentary and advertising.

Throughout all of this, Adams cultivates a wry humour and witty awareness that make the film accessible, and then, reflexively apprehensive of what and how such 'accessibility' is enabled. The film is invoking a constant and anxious parallel in media strategies of pathos, narrative and association. In perhaps one of the most memorable sections, the visual seemingly disappears altogether leaving a black screen and white text – playing with voiceover and its tensions with text (and textual inconsistency) to compel and question rhythms of attention. It is an attention that moves into, and with, turns of humour; in this sequence, the voiceover's vignette seasons its dark account of an attempted overdose in McDonalds with throwaway puns: "one of his hang-ups was telephones". Combining an acute and characterful manipulation of language and sound, alongside film and video manipulation, Adams' work has been screened widely and abroad since 1982. His work is held in major collections, including: Museum of Modern Art, New York; Centre Georges Pompidou, Paris; Art Gallery of New South Wales; BBC and National Gallery of Ontario. *Intellectual Properties* has been revisited recently, screening in Tyneside Cinema's Gallery (24th May – 18th June, 2017), offering a chance to engage again with this rewarding, playful and worryingly relevant moment in British experimental film.

DS

Could you say a bit about your involvement in the Newcastle-based art collective 'The Basement Group'? Beyond the programmed events (of which there were apparently over 230!) did the group have a presiding aesthetic or particular artistic approach, and did this extend to political/social objectives?

JA

There's a lot of history between then and now. I studied fine art at Newcastle Polytechnic between 1976 and 1979. It was an extraordinary time to be a student there. Many of the lecturers were visionary and forward looking, inviting a swathe of visiting practitioners from a number of disciplines. It so happened also that my year group was very strong. I recall that there were 9 firsts in that cohort on graduation, something that had not happened before. Some of those students working in performance and video art were encouraged by lecturers Roger Wilson and Stuart Marshall, to set up an exhibition space, following the demise of the Ayton Basement. And so the Basement Group formed. We presented a wide range of work by students, emerging and established artists.

Generally speaking, much of that work was ephemeral, questioning the notion of art as commodity and the values of broadcast television at the time. The Basement Group evolved into Projects UK and subsequently Locus Plus, which still operates today as an internationally respected commissioning agency. Throughout, the organisation has been led by Jon Bewley, who appears in *Intellectual Properties* as the commentator on copyright. My own involvement over the years has been largely peripheral, serving on the board of trustees.

DS

Throughout your films (I'm thinking here specifically of **Sensible Shoes***, 1983,* **Intellectual Properties***, 1985, and* **Goldfish Memoirs***, 1993) there is a reflexive preoccupation with film and/or video as a way to draw attention to how mercurial the* *same image(s) can be…always contingent, shifting in relation to sound, voice, text and context. Yet, rather than this being a structuralist tool interrogating the medium or a deconstruction of film-as-material, your repeated or re-visited rhythms of foot-age seem more engaged with just how vulnerable the viewer is to narrative and its suggestion. In* **Intellectual Properties** *we encounter the term 'Mediaocracy' and each chapter of the work is followed by the advertising quip "We'll be back after these messages…" To what extent do you feel that the film's anxiety around media representation, and the contexts of image manipulation, was specific to its time of making, in the 80s… and how, for you, has it changed and escalated?*

JA

Anyone who works in film and video, is naturally interested in the nature and properties of the media. In the case of the latter particularly, evolution of the form has essentially followed technological development. My contemporaries were largely exploring the properties and limits of the existing technologies, as was I. However, for me that wasn't enough. We are all engaged by stories - telling them, listening to them and sharing them. So I was looking for different ways to tell stories using approaches which were not conventional and certainly not mainstream. It occurred to me that the interpretation of moving images might be influenced and contextualised by the accompanying soundtrack and that by applying this concept in a number of ways, there was an opportunity to create multi-layered narratives.

Arguably, it is the task of the filmmaker to manipulate the feelings and thoughts of the audience and, as an editor, I would always ask myself, 'What is the viewer thinking now?' Encouraging the viewer to modify those thoughts and interpretations, to reflect on and change that thinking during the course of the film, was an interesting notion for me. And that approach applies to the three works that you mention, to a degree. Structurally, to achieve that in *Intellectual Properties*, was a rather complex post-production process - and in fact was pushing the available technology to its limits. So I was definitely concerned with the properties of the medium in that sense.

Regarding the manipulation of the media, I was very interested in that. Immediately before working on *Intellectual*

Properties, I was editing for Trade Films, (one of Channel Four regional workshops at the time) cutting videos supporting the union movement during the miners' strike. The strike was lost in an avalanche of mainstream media propaganda and I was very aware of that. Moving to the USA to make the film, I was looking at the way mainstream media was being employed there. In the more or less the same way of course but overwhelmingly to sell products. It seemed inescapable - and in the land of plenty there was certainly lots of things to buy.

Looking out from the centre of capitalism, I was also thinking a lot about the future. My own, as a struggling artist and more generally the way the world was shaping up. It seemed to me unlikely that I could make a living in this way as the odds were stacked against the creator, for the most part. Hence the theme of copyright and intellectual property. From this viewpoint, it seemed that the world would be governed by business and therefore by privately owned media. I coined the term 'mediaocracy' to frame this and it seems, that is the way things have turned out. So in answer to your question, media rules - but interestingly it is social media which we have happily allowed to invade our private lives. Without coercion we seem willing and able to let the world know everything about us. So Orwell was a little wide of the mark I suppose. He couldn't have guessed that 1984 would be the year that Mark Zuckerberg was born. When this bright spark conceived Facebook at Harvard, he probably was thinking more about getting laid than becoming Big Brother. But that's the way it has turned out.

DS

Watching **Intellectual Properties** *now in 2017 has a lot of disarmingly uncanny points of resonance for a contemporary audience: you have a gun-toting celebrity (John Wayne) reincarnated to run for presidency as a hologram; a vignette about banks collapsing and public funding of the arts; a company that delivers awkward or distressing phone calls on behalf of people, introducing corporate service into personal interaction; and surveillance, detachment and acting become the default states of a paranoid existence. There is also a sense in which the music and footage seem to play into current nostalgic obsessions with past versions of the future, the synth-squelch* *sci-fi of yesterday's tomorrow…consequently* **Intellectual Properties** *seems to speak simultaneously to much of today's concerns and to equally evoke film and media's current turn to the 70s/80s in their varying and often sickly venerations of the retro. Since making the film have you been tempted to return to its increasingly prescient ideas for other projects?*

JA

The preoccupation with a vague retro past in music and film is a rather depressing notion. As if the ideas bag is somehow empty. It would be rather exciting to see a revolution in either medium and I think that it is long overdue. On the other hand, there is plenty of game-changing going on in the fields of science and technology. We are on the edge of something that will give many of us a bumpy ride. In self driven cars that we won't own probably. Developments in artificial intelligence and robotics will have a major impact on society in the next 30 years and we can see already that social media is shaping politics and the cultural climate. Encouragingly, it appears too that for the young at least, the days of tabloid newspapers moulding public opinion are over.

So there is plenty to think about and speculate on. Witness the young couple on the sofa. She is wondering where the relationship is going and says to him, 'Don't you think that it's time we had a discussion about the future?' He says, 'What, you mean about flying cars and all that?'

DS

Could you talk through some of your points of influence for the film? Were there any British filmmakers at the time that interested you – or more literary/textual points of reference?

JA

There are plenty of British filmmakers and artists that I admire but I can't say that they influenced me directly. The work of Jean-Luc Godard and Chris Marker stood out for me as a student and Michael Snow's *Wavelength* seemed to be a rather important film also. Probably writers have a greater impact on my thinking; Kurt Vonnegut and Haruki Murakami come to mind.

The latter being one of the great living writers I think. *The Magus* by John Fowles was in mind whilst I was making *Intellectual Properties*. Bob Dylan's words and music have been in my head since I was 13, so there is no doubt that my output has been slanted by his way of looking at the world.

DS

The film uses footage from both Newcastle and Boston, returning often to the outsider figure journeying...could you talk a bit about your experiences filming in America? Did you get a sense of any particular art communities while you were over there, or discover anything in particular that has fed into your creative practice?

JA

Intellectual Properties was made possible by a grant from Massachusetts Council on the Arts and Humanities. A condition of the grant was that the work should be produced there. It was my first visit to the US and I was very fortunate to be offered accommodation with a talented and connected artist, Jane Gillooly. Jane introduced me to the wider community of artists and musicians in Boston and Cambridge. I was grateful to be welcomed by that mutually supportive group, many of whom contributed to the film and a few years later to a second more ambitious project, *Jamaica Plain*. I was treated very kindly as a guest there and subsequently drove across the country twice, generally finding a particular generosity of spirit in American people. However, I also became very aware of my own Englishness, something that I had never thought about before. I think that cultural difference informed *Intellectual Properties* and later work also.

DS

In the section entitled 'Medioacracy', a voiceover relates the scenario of a therapist and her patient, a writer, and within this narrative the voiceover then follows a second narrative in which through meandering attention the writer recalls an attempted overdose in a McDonald's toilet (on a literal seat of capitalism).

It is perhaps the film's most immediate and compelling section, despite there being no images – only white text on black. The style of prose feels consciously American, in an almost hard-boiled meets anecdotal/beat manner…were there any particular writers or scenarios you were drawing from here?

JA

Well, I had read Kerouac, Burroughs, Ken Kesey, Tom Wolfe, Vonnegut and so on before then, so subconsciously any of those might have influenced the style. Elmore Leonard too perhaps. Who knows? We all pick up stuff as we go along and it lodges there in some part of the brain. But consciously no. Reagan was president then, graduating from acting to politics with ease. I was thinking about that, wondering if he was really just a performer delivering the lines written for him. It was then that I began looking into the life of John Wayne, the now deceased Hollywood actor who seemed to embody the idea of the great American hero. Eventually after all of that musing one day it all came out on the page. Others say that they don't know where writing comes from - as if the writer was just some kind of conduit - that rings true for me and I think that is certainly true of that story.

'Mediaocracy' was narrated by an American (Jane Gillooly) so I was aiming for an authenticity of voice and phrasing. I asked Jane to check the script and advise me on that. For example, Percodan, the drug used in the overdose, was at the time the drug of choice for suicide attempts in the US at the time and 'Drop Kick Me Jesus Through the Goalposts of Life' was the corniest country and Western song title she could think of. I couldn't though, quite bring myself to spell words like 'colour' in the American way.

It was a little sci-fi story really, taking a punt at a future possibility. That future hasn't quite happened yet but It seems quite possible that one day there will be a holographic president - or a robot. We aren't that far from it really. The word 'Mediaocracy' came to me as a term which might describe the state of things in that particular world. Thirty odd years later we now live in one, certainly.

DS

There are moments of disjunction between the text and voiceover – where the heard voice will betray the seen text – can you talk a bit about this process and how it might relate to revealing the tactics of narrative – what is said and what is implied? With the overarching 'narrative', or organizing principle, of **Intellectual Properties** *being copyright, does the text and voiceover offer a different angle specific to language? The writer's problem is, as the voiceover assures us, 'he had absolutely nothing to say', and yet, departing from the voiceover, the text at that point reads 'he had committed the sin of plagiarism'...*

JA

It was an experiment, something that I hadn't seen done before. I was surprised by the psychological effect of overlaying voice with text. I was playing around with the timing and displacement of words and voice initially, then introducing mismatches between the two, silences, blank screens and so on. Stuff designed to encourage the viewer to pay attention.

Regarding the specific example, plagiarism remains a cardinal sin in the creative community. A breach of intellectual property. Worse of course, if you are found out. My Sweet Lord, I hope it never happens to me.

DS

The situation of psychoanalysis reoccurs in **Goldfish Memoirs** *(1993) in which one of the interviewees describes psychoanalysis as a damaging way to negotiate the past, the film also describes the clichés of a self-help tape and interviews a psychologist on her interest in delusions. Returning to* **Intellectual Properties**, *the therapy scene is introduced with the text: 'She doesn't believe in the couch | for her, analysis should be | a cinematic experience'...to what extent do you agree with this? The recurrent presence of psychoanalysis (in both* **Goldfish Memoirs** *and* **Intellectual Properties***) is paired with the significance of memory, I was wondering, along with the use of photographs and concepts of journeying, is this a point of connection with the films of Chris Marker?*

Psychoanalysis had its origins over 100 years ago but when I first visited US in 1984, the idea of voluntarily undergoing therapy seemed to be a purely American preoccupation. The possibility that a working class bloke from Yorkshire would indulge in something like that would be laughable. Of course, what happens over there eventually happens here and so it has. I'm not sure whether any practitioner uses film as a tool to explore the psyche but if the question is could psychoanalysis be a cinematic experience, then I would say why not? In the story, however that was just a device to introduce John Wayne, who starred in *Red River* the film being shown in the session. The film incidentally was the subject of a lawsuit by Howard Hughes, against producer/director Howard Hawks. Hughes claimed that Hawks plagiarized a scene from an earlier film *The Outlaw* and forced a re-edit prior to release.

As I later discovered, a fundamental of psychoanalysis is the exploration of memory, one of my abiding interests. So in *Goldfish Memoirs*, a film about bipolar disorder, it was natural to explore themes of memory and analysis. Chris Marker's film *Sans Soleil* is an exploration of memory and the human condition, so to some extent there is a connection between that and *Goldfish Memoirs*.

DS

A recognisable trait in all of your works is the presence of humour, through dry anecdotal wit or in protracted jokes there seems to be a continual and wry comedy at play. Sometimes, through puns or comic (mis)hearing, you seem to draw parallels between jokes as constructed and artificial devices and the trappings or manipulation of narrative – could you say a bit about these elements in your work?

JA

I am very fond of using irony, humour and jokes in my work. Specifically, jokes have a particular relevance in *Intellectual Properties* in that they are passed around and shared freely. Generally, they are not subject to copyright and have long been viral before the term was coined in the modern context. Many jokes are also constructed to deceive and misdirect an audience, so it seemed appropriate to include them in a film which manipulates the viewer in a similar way. Humour often has a way of encouraging us to reflect on the human condition and perhaps Intellectual Properties makes some efforts in that direction.

DS

You recently completed an MA in Creative Writing at Newcastle University...I would be fascinated to know what you think of 'Creativity' as a taught and institutionalised discipline, given the reflective nature of your engagement with creativity in your films: appearing, as it does, in tension with the concept of a profession – in relation to commerce, politics, funding, and mental well-being. How does writing and film relate for you, as they are both clearly fundamental to your creativity?

JA

I have to say that I enjoyed the Creative Writing course immensely. For me it reaffirmed the fact that I could derive great joy from making up stories, from sometimes managing to put down appropriate words in the right order. However, the major lesson learned during that period of study, was how very difficult it is to make a living from writing. The tutors at Newcastle are highly talented and respected authors, poets and playwrights, yet they necessarily have to teach in order to survive. Nothing wrong with that of course and in my case I had no particular ambition to become a financially successful writer.

Regarding the question of whether creativity can be taught in any particular institution, I would doubt that. However, it can be encouraged and developed in the right environment, any kind of education is a good thing as far as I am concerned. For me writing, filmmaking and ceramics - which I studied for some years - are all part of the same thing. A desire to make stuff and say something to the world.

DS

What projects are you working on at the moment – and do they continue to move between the linguistic (and/or literary) and the cinematic?

JA

After half a lifetime of making videos and multimedia for commercial clients perhaps it is time to return to art for art's sake. There is a half-written novel that I have to finish and I'm trying to solve some technical/software issues in order to make a new video installation. But what I really want to do is build a straw bale house.

[2017]

A N D R E W K Ö T T I N G

The first film I saw by Andrew Kötting was *This, Our Still Life* (2011). After the film finished, I had that rare and fluttering excitement that what I had just watched would far outlive the duration of my viewing. I had watched the film on DVD in a flat in London. On leaving the dark room and out into the street I began to immediately walk towards the BFI Southbank where I knew they had a copy of his first feature *Gallivant* (1996). It was one of those moments where, walking beneath an unnervingly blue sky and in the giddy aftermath of what I'd just seen, everything seemed bustling for my attention, each thing more vividly itself and newly awake to (re)discovery. Striding forth to purchase another skittish dose of Kötting, bounding after my next fix, caught up in its afterglow – gratefully infected – seeing within and from its restless energy, following its propulsive curiosity.

Taking a mutable form somewhere between documentary, collage, film-essay and a playfully diaristic recording as the basis for a visual poetics, *This, Our Still Life* centres around Kötting's family (specifically his daughter Eden, who has a rare genetic disorder, Joubert's Syndrome) as they spend time in a remote part-time home in the Pyrenees. Taking cues from the changing seasons, the old farmhouse (deeply and romantically isolated amid forest and mountain) becomes a rickety locus for family rituals: the daily struggles, frustrations, intimacies, and joys that build a life and its collaborative explorations in and as art. The film is edited with Kötting's characteristic jumps of intuition and scattershot logic; itching with humour and eccentric seriousness, its handheld kineticism eager to be out and among the accidents of happening. In this unstill 'still-life' portrait (if 'portrait' is in turn the departure for makeshift galleries of moving), the film's distracted zest for observation and personal family-footage begins to perfectly enact a defining focus for Kötting's filmography: the spaces between 'outsider' and 'insider-art'; between art, performance, living and film; between a collaged poetics and a filmed journey; and between people and landscape.

This interview took place after I met Andrew for a Q&A at Tyneside Cinema, he was introducing Edith Walks. The film (like his films *Gallivant*, *Swandown* and *By Our Selves*) took the form of a journey. A walk-in dialogue with the spirit of Edith Swanneck, stepped out in séance between Hastings and Waltham Abbey to reunite the dismembered, battle-torn body of King Harold with his wife. Undertaken as an improvised pilgrimage, the film curates a troop of fellow musicians, historians and writers, bringing together: the bearded gnosticism of Alan Moore, the conspiracy of literary cartography that is Iain Sinclair, the musical innovations of Jem Finer, and the incarnation of Edith in Claudia Barton – a singer clad in an increasingly bedraggled dress. The film was accompanied by a beautiful book (*EDITH The Chronicles*) , a CD of field recordings and music, and touring performances alongside screenings.

Andrew's responses came in the emphatic shout of caps-lock, reminding me of the text in *This, Our Still Life*, I kept it that way as I feel it is in-keeping with the spirit of a 'dirt-under-the-fingernails' bounding, climbing and swimming that runs throughout all of his work...BOLD ELEMENTS OF LANGUAGE UNTETHERED / GATHERED / LAUGHING / LIGHT / WALK-ING / DRUMS UP / & ONWARDS...

DS

*Whether it is in puncturing the hubris of Pound's cantos with a small plastic swan (****Swandown***, 2012), retracing the pilgrimage of John Clare (****By Our Selves***, 2015) or exhuming the lines of Heinrich Heine via strolling song (****Edith's Walk***, 2017), poetry continually excerpts an influence or presence in your films...are there any particular poets that you read for pleasure, or that are particularly significant to you? Do you read much contemporary poetry?*

AK

I READ POETRY INTERMITTENTLY – BUT INVARIABLY IF IT'S FOISTED UPON ME I'M RESISTANT TO IT – WE DID A LOT OF WORDSWORTH AND KEATS AT SCHOOL – HOWEVER I HAVE SHARED A STUDIO WITH A POET AND PUBLISHER OF POETRY FOR ALMOST EIGHT YEARS NOW SO A LOT OF HIS ENTHUSIAM HAS RUBBED OFF ON ME – I LIKE THE METAPHYSICAL WEIGHT OF POETRY – THE NEED TO DIG INTO IT – BUT ALSO ITS IMMEDIACY WHEN IT WORKS.

I USED TO LIKE TO STUMBLE ACROSS POETRY – WHEN I WAS GROWING UP IT WOULD HAVE BEEN

RICHARD BRAUTIGAN – SAMUEL BECKETT AND JOHN COOPER CLARK BUT MORE RECENTLY IT'S KAE TEMPEST MEREDITH MONK MARGARET ATWOOD AND NICK CAVE – AND THEN OF COURSE JOHN CLARE – LUCKILY I WAS BULLIED MERCILESSLY INTO RESEARCHING HIS WORK BECAUSE OF A PROJECT I WAS INVOLVED WITH - *BY OUR SELVES* - PROFESSOR SIMON KOVESI WOULD KEEP BOMBARDING ME WITH 'STUFF' – HE'S A CLAREHEAD - THE ASYLUM POEMS ARE VERY POWERFUL AND INSPIRING – IAIN SINCLAIR HAS OBVIOUSLY BEEN A BIG INFLUENCE AND ALSO BRIAN CATLING.

TODAY I FIND MYSELF TRAVELLING WITH THE WRITINGS OF E.M CIORAN; 'THE TROUBLE WITH BEING BORN' 'ON THE HEIGHTS OF DESPAIR' 'THE TEMPTATION TO EXIST' 'A SHORT HISTORY OF DECAY' – THE TITLES THEMSELVES ARE LIKE HAIKU POEMS AND THEN THERE'S DAVID SHIELD'S BOOK 'REALITY HUNGER' – I NEVER TIRE OF DIPPING IN AND OUT OF IT – BUT IT'S NOT 'PROPER' POETRY.

I WRITE A LOT OF PROSE POEMS MYSELF AND INVARIABLY THEY FIND THEIR WAY INTO PROJECTS THAT I'M WORKING ON; PERFFORMANCES/FILMS/ BOOKWORKS/WALL TEXTS AND MY DAUGHTERS COLLAGES AND PAINTINGS

DS

Through using sound as collage and with an ongoing collaboration with Jem Finer (and subsequent albums of field recordings), many of your films seem to suggest a kind of sonic poetics. I'm thinking here of the detailed, careful (dis)arrangement of voices, the hauntings of one film's audio in another's (Gladys and Eden's voices from **Gallivant** *as recalled in* **Swandown***, or the short film,* **Klipperty Klopp***, 1984, echoed by a character in* **Ivul***, 2009, who utters the phrase in joking imitation of a horse), and then the mischievous way in which sound will often complicate or confuse the image. Do you collect sound as part of a project, in a comparable way to accruing footage, or is there a more specific method? Are there particular archives you return to, to gleefully pillage and* *plunder? Do you approach the cutting up and editing of sound as a kind of poetics, embodying and furthering a mode of 'expanded cinema'?*

AK

YES – YOUR QUESTION(S) AND ASSUMPTIONS ARE VERY CLOSE TO REVEALING MY METHODOLOGY; SONIC POETICS/MUSIC CONCRÈTE/MEDIATED COLLAGIC CHAOS/DRIFT POEMS/CHOREOGRAPHED SOUND/IMAGE SCAPES AND 'SPILLAGE' - I'M ALWAYS REVISITING WORKS – LOOKING TO RE-IMAGINE/ RE-WORK/RE-CONFIGURE/RE-ARRANGE/RE-ALLIGN AND RE-GURGITATE BOTH OLD AND NEW FOOTAGE WHETHER IT BE MOVING IMAGE OR SOUND.

'PILLAGE AND PLUNDER' MAKES IT SOUND TOO BRUTAL – I'D LIKE TO THINK THAT THERE'S MORE FINESSE INVOLVED – A NUANCE OF STRUCTURE – AN EBBING AND FLOWING OF IDEAS – A TIDE OF UNDULATING 'IMPLIED' OR 'FRAGMENTED' NARRATIVES – THEMES AND SCHEMES BUT NOTHING TOO DIDACTIC OR OBVIOUS.

I LOVE SUBSTRATA AND SUBTEXT – I LOVE THE INFINITE POSSIBILTIES OF REVERSE ENGINEERING - I ALSO LOVE ATMOSPHERE - I WAS VERY INFLUENCED BY DUB REGGAE WHEN I WAS PRETENDING TO BE A PUNK – I NEVER FOUND THE 1 2 3 SHOUTY SHOUTY WAY OF MAKING MUSIC THAT SATISFYING – ALBEIT THAT I WAS QUITE GOOD AT IT AND CAN STILL DO IT TODAY - BUT ONCE I DISCOVERED THE POTENTIAL OF TAPE LOOPS/REVERB/ DELAY AND ECHO SUDDENLY I WAS UP AND RUNNING INTO THAT WORLD OF 'HAUNTOLOGY' - AS IT HAS MORE RECENTLY BEEN DESCRIBED - YOU CERTAINLY DIDN'T HAVE TO BE A MUSICIAN TO 'MAKE MUSIC' AND JEM FINER HAS ALWAYS BEEN VERY SUPPORTIVE AND REASSURING IN MY ATTEMPTS TO 'MAKE MUSIC'.

I AM ALSO VERY INTERESTED IN MOVING IMAGE ARCHIVE – I HAVE A STRONG RELATIONSHIP WITH SCREEN ARCHIVE SOUTH EAST AT THE UNIVERSITY IN BRIGHTON – I SPEND A COUPLE OF DAYS A YEAR

CATCHING UP ON NEW AQUISITIONS – IT'S MAIN-
LY HOME MOVIES THAT HAVE BEEN BEQUEATHED
IN THE WAKE OF A FAMILY DEATH – 9.5MM/8MM/SU-
PER 8MM/16MM - SOMETIMES EVEN VHS AND THERE
IS DAVID LEISTER - WHEN I WAS LIVING IN LONDON
– WE WOULD HEAD OUT TO THE BFI IN BEACONS-
FIELD AND SALVAGE ANY 16MM PUBLIC INFORMATION
FILMS THAT THEY MIGHT BE THROWING OUT TO
MAKE WAY FOR THE NEW HARD DRIVES – IT WAS LIKE
CHRISTMAS – AND DAVID STILL HAS MASSES OF THAT
STUFF SCATTERED ACROSS LONDON IN VARIOUS LOCK
UPS BATHROOMS AND KITCHENS – I CONSOLIDATED
MY COLLECTION WHEN I ARRIVED IN HASTINGS 15
YEARS AGO BY TRANSFERRING MOST OF THE SOUND
TRACKS FROM A STEENBECK ONTO DAT TAPES OR MORE
RECENTLY MY iPHONE.

DS

*You seem very attentive to the movement between
repetition and play, where 'play' offers interpretive mobility
in addition to valuing child-like perception (whatever that can
or could encompass) and 'repetition' suggests and disrupts
patterns in each film, as a process in which context can re-
configure meaning. Does this changeable, open and chance-
led approach interact with your 'eARTHOUSE Manifesto'?*

AK

REPETITION IS IMPORTANT – AS IS PLAY AND OF
COURSE COMEDY – I THINK DADA IS A PART OF MY DNA
– PERHAPS IT'S THE GERMAN GENES – IT ALSO SERVES
TO DISRUPT ANY POTENTIAL GRAVITAS OR SELF-
IMPORTANCE - IT ALLOWS FOR OTHER WAYS OF
SEEING OR HEARING – CONTEXT IS THEREFORE
GIVEN THE CHANCE TO BE READ DIFFERENTLY AND
THUS AMBIGUITY COMES INTO PLAY – WHICH I'M A
VERY BIG FAN OF – IT'S EASY TO GET LOST THOUGH
AND OCCASIONALLY I RESORT TO A REPETITION-OF –
ATTEMPT BY WAY OF TRYING THINGS AGAIN BUT IN A
DIFFERENT ORDER!

THE EARTHOUSE MANIFESTO WAS WRITTEN WITH MY TONGUE FIRMLY IN MY CHEEK AS A REACTION TO THE DOGME MANIFESTO WHICH HAD JUST COME OUT – I THINK BOTH MANIFESTOS REMIND US THAT THERE ARE OTHER WAYS OF MAKING WORK OUTSIDE OF THE INDUSTRIAL NORMS – BUT FOR COLLEAGUES AND FELLOW PRACTITIONERS THAT WORK OUTSIDE OF THE MAINSTREAM FILM GULAG - WE ALL KNEW THIS BUT IT WAS GOOD TO BE REMINDED AND HAVE IT WRITTEN DOWN – AND OF COURSE THERE WAS THE JUSTIFICATION FOR ME TO GET MY ARMS OR FEET INSIDE ANOTHER SENTIENT BEING, ALIVE OR DEAD…

DS

It seems like this would be a good point to question the significance of what is left unfinished or unresolved in your films. Looping and meandering, the films (like the journeys they depict) often enact a restless structuring that permits no final structure but that is left open to continue – a continuing – a going-on…I was wondering how much of this was linked to your reading of Beckett or E.M Cioran…or other bleak advocates of the fragment, the decay and the endless unanswered…

AK

I THINK THEIR WRITING HAS HAD A PROFOUND IMPACT – THE WRITING IS OPEN FOR INTERPRETATION AND MEANING – I ENJOY THE NOTION OF FLUX OR CONTINGENCY – THINGS AREN'T FIXED – THINGS AREN'T 'NORMAL' IN THEIR STRUCTURE.

THE BIRTH OF MY DAUGHTER **EDEN** – THROUGH HER PROFOUND DISABILITY HAS ALSO 'ENABLED' ME – SHE HAS INSPIRED ME AND THWARTED ME – MOVED ME AND ANNIHILATED ME – BECAUSE OF HER I NEVER BECAME THE PERSON THAT I THOUGHT/HOPED I MIGHT BECOME – SHE CONTINUES TO TEACH ME ABOUT ENDURANCE/HUMILITY/HOPE AND DESPONDENCY – SHE PUSHES ME INTO TROUGHS OF MELANCHOLY ONLY TO THEN HELP ME SOAR INTO THE REALMS OF SUBLIMITY – SHE HAS NURTURED MY LOVE OF BOTH

THE PHYSICAL AND THE METAPHYSICAL – LIKE A MUSE
OR ILL ADVISED CONFIDENT….
   BUT ALWAYS THE GOING-ON…

DS

Despite the improvisation and play that animates much of each
film, there is also, it seems, an interest and investment in rit-
ual, or versions of the ritualistic. This is apparent throughout
your work: from the early and incredible **Hub Bub in Baöbabs**
(1989) and the folkloric anthropology of **Gallivant** *(1996);*
the chain of site-specific, inflated tributes of **In the Wake of**
Deadad *(2006); and through to the re-traced journeys,*
honouring and speculating upon obscured histories, in **By**
Our Selves *(2015) and* **Edith Walks** *(2017). It feels as though*
a kind of 'ritual' might also apply to the significance of collab-
oration, of gathering and constellating like-minded people?
Or perhaps even your continued gravitation towards acts of
endurance, of making the film a physical, as well as artistic,
endeavour (or erasing those distinctions) …this also seems
connected to a ritualised impulse. Would you agree that non-
religious ritual is something that consciously shapes your
approach?

AK

YES – A PRE-CHRISTIAN ANTI-MONOTHEISTIC
APPROACH IS VERY IMPORTANT – IT'S ONLY DURING
THE LAST TEN YEARS THAT I'VE ATTEMPTED TO ARTIC-
ULATE MY LOATHING AND DREAD OF 'THE BIG-BOOK-
IST-BRAIN-WASHERS' – A MALE DOMINATED/ALL POW-
ERFUL/SUPERSTITIOUS/ANTI-HUMANISTIC APPROACH
OF CONTROLLING FREEDOM OF SPIRIT – I LOVE
THE FOLKLORIC – THE METAPHOR OF MYTHOLOGY
AND THE POWER OF RITUAL – THE MARRIAGE OF
THE CORPOREAL AND 'REAL' EXPERIENCE WITH
THAT OF THE CEREBRAL – THE CONTEMPLATIVE
MEDITATIVE POWER OF BEING-IN-LANDSCAPE – THE
MULLING OF DEEP TIME – AS ARTICULATED
BY JEM FINER'S 1,000 YEAR-LONG MUSIC
COMPOSITION LONGPLAYER OR ALAN MOORE'S

THINKING…. THE SHAMANISTIC POTENTIAL IN ALL OF US IS SOMETHING THAT I'M ALSO INTERESTED IN.

SO THE WORKS ARE CONSISTENTLY CONCEIVED WITH ENDURANCE OR JOURNEYING AS A CATALYST OR AMBIITION AND THIS IS SOMETHING THAT IAIN SINCLAIR HAS BEEN DOING FOR A VERY LONG TIME – WE CONNECTED WHEN I MOVED TO HASTINGS AND FOUND A WAY TO CELEBRATE OUR KINDRED SPIRITEDNESS THROUGH COLLABORATION – HIS GENEROSITY OF MIND RE-CHARGED MY BATTERIES AND TOOK THE WORK INTO A DIRECTION THAT I HAD INTUITIVELY BEEN DABBLING WITH WHEN I MADE *JAUNT* AND *GALLIVANT* BUT NOT FULLY REALISED - HIS MORE RECENT PROSE MANAGES TO CONSTRUCT POETIC THOUGHTSCAPES USING JUST WORDS TO GREAT EFFECT – I FIND THEM SPELLBINDING - MY PROCESS INVOLVES MOVING IMAGE/SPOKEN WORD/ SOUND AND MUSIC BUT ULTIMATELY I'M ALSO TRYING TO CAST SPELLS.

IT IS THROUGH COLLABORATION THOUGH THAT MUCH OF THE WORK ATTAINS ITS MAGIC AND POTENTIAL – I'VE ALWAYS WORKED WITH PEOPLE THAT I HAVE A FONDNESS FOR REGARDLESS OF WHETHER THEY ARE 'GOOD AT THEIR JOB' OR 'PROFESSIONAL' – IT IS MORE ABOUT RELATIONSHIPS AND BEING-ABLE-TO-SPEND-TIME-TOGETHER – SOME OF THOSE EARLI-ER COLLABORATORS HAVE DRIFTED AWAY BUT THAT INVARIABLY HAS MORE TO DO WITH GEOGRAPHICAL DISTANCE – ALTHOUGH IN A FEW INSTANCES IT HAS ALSO HAD SOMETHING TO DO WITH A MEANESS -OF-SPIRIT IN THEIR AMBITION FOR WANTING ME TO BECOME MORE MAINSTREAM AND ACCESIBLE.

DS

Following on from the mention of endurance, I was won-dering whether you are ever tempted to explore the viewer's endurance? It seems that, whilst your own endur-ance or pursuit of physical and feet-on-the-ground experience (extending to those around you in the filming process) is paramount, the films do not necessarily demand a reciprocal endurance in the viewer... in terms of shot-length and duration (a slowness that emerges, say, in Ben Rivers' work), or the resistance of abrasive imagery or uncomfortable visuals... do these cinematic approaches interest you at all?

AK

THEY DO AND WITH BEN'S WORK IN PARTICULAR – I THINK WE ARE BARKING UP A SIMILAR TREE BUT BEN IS BRAVER WHEN IT COMES TO THE DURATIONAL – HE'S VERY INTO THE MATERIALITY OF FILM - OF CELLULOID – I BLAME IT ON THE FACT THAT HE HAND PROCESSES MUCH OF THE WORK AS WELL AS THE LENGTH OF A HAND CRANK TO A 16MM BOLEX.

A LOT OF MY EARLIER WORK WAS A PRETTY HARDCORE BARRAGE OF SOUND AND IMAGE – MY RYTHMS WERE ERRATIC AND AT TIMES TOURETTES-LIKE – I'VE SLOWED DOWN AS I'VE GOT OLDER LOOKING FOR A DIFFERENT ORDER – AND I'VE NEVER BEEN AFRAID OF 'UNCOMFORTABLE VISUALS' - WORKS LIKE *ANVIL-HEAD THE HUN/FLESHFILM/NUCLEUS AMBIGOUS/ME/ABOVE THEM THE WORLD BEYOND* AND *THIS FILTHY EARTH* - I THINK MY NEW FILM *LEK AND THE DOGS* IS QUITE AN UNCOMFORTABLE RIDE IN PLACESBUTTHEIMAGESAREMEDIATEDTHROUGHALESS ERRATIC VIEWING EXPERIENCE – IT FEELS LIKE A HYBRID; A PIECE OF WORK IN WHICH THE JOURNEYWORKS; *GALLIVANT/SWANDOWN/BY OURSELVES/ EDITH WALKS* MERGE WITH THE AMBITION OF THE STORYWORKS; *THIS FILTHY EARTH* AND *IVUL.*

DS

Having just said asked about 'abrasive imagery' and the possibility of uncomfortable viewing experiences, I have just remembered two of your short films that do delve into this area: **Me** *(2000) and* **Above Them the World Beyond** *(2013). Both of these films, in very different ways, approach frightening levels of discomfort and make for challenging, and impressively* *unhinged, viewing. Do you find yourself drawn to darker implications and sequences in your films and then having to later cut back, or edit out (as with **Me**, which was originally to be included in **Gallivant**)?*

AK

I THINK I'VE EXPANDED ON SOME OF THIS WITH THE ANSWER TO THE PREVIOUS QUESTION – BUT YES I'M ALWAYS REVISITING WORKS – LOOKING TO RE-IMAGINE/RE-WORK/RE-CONFIGURE/RE-ARRANGE/ RE-ALLIGN/RE-GURGITATE OLD AND NEW FOOTAGE WHETHER IT BE MOVING IMAGE OR SOUND – OLD AND NEW ANSWERS ARE NO EXCEPTION!

DS

*To what extent you see your films as an extension of performance-art…or the documentation of performance art? I feel as though the suits you wear (**In the Wake of Deadad /
Swandown / Edith Walks**) signal the initiation, in costume, of a performance or persona…or is 'the suit' (in its changing guises) perhaps another instance of ritual?*

AK

MUCH OF THE WORK IS ROOTED IN PERFORMANCE ART – I WAS BESOTTED BY JOSEPH BEUYS STAURT BRISLEY AND GINA PANE WHEN I WAS AT ART SCHOOL – THERE WAS AN ATMOSPHERE ABOUT THEIR WORK – THEY PERFORMED MAINLY FOR THE GALLERY SPACE BUT MY ANTICS WITHIN THE PUBLIC SPACE HAVE PROVID-ED RICH MATERIAL FOR BOTH THE INSTALLATIONS/ FILMS/PERFORMANCES THAT I MAKE THEREAFTER - THE SUIT REPRESENTS A MINDSET OR CHARACTER – AN INVITATION TO ENJOY THE RIDICULOUSNESS OF AMBITION AND BY INHABITING THE SUIT I FIND MYSELF COCOONED OR COMFORTED – A PROTECTION – I THINK IT WAS INSPIRED BY BOTH MY GERMAN GRAND FATHER WHO WOULD ALWAYS BE MENDING THE CAR OR GARDENING IN HIS THREE PIECE SUIT OR THE FILM

THE MOON AND THE SLEDGEHAMMER – I LOVED THE IDEA OF THE MEN OF THE PAGE FAMILY WEARING SUITS WHILST HARD-AT-WORK IN THE LANDSCAPE – IT FELT INCONGOROUS AND EXCITING - ON ANOTHER MORE MUNDANE LEVEL IT ALSO MEANS THAT I NEVER HAVE TO THINK ABOUT WHAT TO PUT ON IN THE MORNING.

DS

I was wondering if you could say a bit about the Earth trilogy? With **This Filthy Earth** *(2001) you mutated elements from John Berger's* **Pig Earth** *and Zola's* **La Terre** *to create a mud-soaked community wed to the earth, and in* **Ivul** *(2009) a fractured family leads to a young boy's self-imposed exile from touching the earth – into an existence in the treetops. Is* **Lek and the Dogs** *the final in this proposed trilogy? Do you feel much has changed in your practice from the first 'Earth-instalment' to now, with its completion in sight?*

AK

I TOUCHED ON THIS IN THE ANSWER TO AN EARLIER QUESTION BUT INDEED A LOT HAS CHANGED FROM WHEN I MADE *THIS FILTHY EARTH* – TO MAKE THAT 'TYPE OF FILM' TODAY WOULD BE A LOT HARDER – AT THE TIME I WAS SEDUCED BY ALL THE ATTENTION I WAS BEING PAID IN THE WAKE OF THE SUCCESS OF *GALLIVANT* AND ALSO A SELF-CONFIDENCE OF BEING ABLE TO 'TELL-A-STORY' ON A GRANDER SCALE WITHIN A POETIC (MADE-UP) LANDSCAPE – I WOULD HAVE BEEN LOST WITHOUT THE SUPPORT OF SEAN LOCK WHO WROTE IT WITH ME – BUT UL-TIMATELY THE FILM IS A FRAGMENTED NARRATIVE DELIVERED WITH A WANTON DISREGARD TO THE COVENANTS OF CONVENTIONAL CINEMATIC STORY TELLING – I REMEMBER SEAN COMING OUT OF THE FINAL SCREENING WITH HIS HEAD IN HIS HANDS BEMOANING; 'WHAT THE FUCK HAVE YOU DONE?' – I DID IT AGAIN WITH *IVUL* – ALWAYS LOOKING TO REVERSE ENGINEER NEW/DIFFERENT MEANING INTO WHATEVER THE PROJECT STARTED OUT AS – IT MUST

BE VERY FRUSTRATING FOR MY COLLABORATORS –
HOWEVER AS THE BODY OF WORK HAS GROWN I THINK
THAT PATTERNS ARE APPEARING THAT WERE MOST
EVIDENT IN MY FIRST PERFORMANCE/LAND ART/PISS
TAKE FILM; *KLIPPERTY KLÖPP* – IN WHICH A MAN (ME) IS
SEEN RUNNING ROUND AND ROUND IN CIRCLES IN THE
LANDSCAPE CARRYING A PAINTING OF A PRE-HISTORIC
HORSE TO THE POINT OF EXHAUSTION – A MONOLOGUE
AS VOICEOVER ATTEMPTS TO MAKE SENSE OF WHAT
IS HAPPENING BUT ULTIMATELY FAILS TO GIVE ANY
RATIONALE OR ORDER TO THE EVENT – IT WAS SHOWN
MANY MOONS BACK AS AN INSTALLATION AT THE
CENTRE POMPIDOU AS PART OF A SAMUEL BECKETT
EXHIBITION WHICH MADE ME HAPPY HAPPY HAPPY –
AND HAS COME TO REPRESENT MANY OF THE THEMES
AND AMBITIONS THAT STILL INFORM MY WORK TODAY.

LEK AND THE DOGS FURTHER DEVELOPS MOST OF
MY PREOCCUPATIONS THROUGH A MONOLOGUE
(INSPIRED BY *KRAPP'S LAST TAPE*)

-   THE THEMES OF ISOLATION/ENDURANCE/
RELIGIOUS BELIEF SYSTEMS/LANDSCAPE/PLACE/
RITUAL/REPETITION/ARCHIVE/ATMOSPHERE/BEASTI-
ALITY/DOGS/ETERNITYAND HOPE

DS

*To return to writing, specifically poetry, you have yourself
written a series of what could be called experimental essays
and prose-poems, many of which accompany your daughter
Eden's art. Beyond a collaborative input with Eden's published
sketchbook, This Illuminated World is Full of Stupid Men (2015-
2016), and the books that accompany your films, do you have
any desire to further publish your writing? How do you view
your own writing? Is it always in service of, or inspired by,
another project...or do you often write as an activity separate
and autonomous from your film and art?*

AK

I'VE NEVER SEPARATED WHAT I DO WITH MY
PROSE-POEMS AND OTHER WRITINGS FROM WHAT I

DO AS AN ARTIST – THEY ARE PATHETIC ONGOING ATTEMPTS AT BEING NOTICED OR REMEMBERED – AT ONCE ONE AND THE SAME AS ALL THE OTHER 'STUFF' THAT I MAKE – I'D LIKE TO THINK THAT AT SOME POINT BEFORE I DIE I MIGHT PUBLISH THEM MYSELF THROUGH **BADBLÖODANDSIBYL** WITH CONTRIBUTIONS FROM AS MANY OF THE PEOPLE THAT I'VE LOVED AND WORKED WITH OVER THE YEARS AS POSSIBLE.

[2017]

LISA SAMUELS

Lisa Samuels is a poet whose work diversely explores and inhabits a plurality of form and impulse: essays, sound art, collaboration, performance, film, theory, philosophy, and the continual intermingling of these fields in ways that energetically refute their distinction. From *LETTERS* (Meow Press, 1996) to *Symphony for Human Transport* (Shearsman, 2017), in the fourteen collections in-between and through editing a recent anthology (*A TransPacific Poetics*, Litmus Press, 2017), Lisa Samuels' engagement with poetry has always upheld a challenging and tireless ability to question and invent. Although it is facile to suggest any one defining characteristic in a poetics that prioritizes the mutable and mobile, it is in the confluence of body and language and the possibility to embody (or be embodied), that Samuels often returns. Syntax becomes a bending gristle of feeling, words are willed into somatic friction, and the page opens itself (as a self and its dissolution) to reacting anatomies of experience. Her poetry is complex, felt, and philosophically realised (without resolution) in the sensory and tactile proof of living, as that living pursues and loses grip and gulp of where and when to ground, in language, what living is.

DS

I want to begin by asking you about the writhingly glorious epic of skin, breath and water that is **Tender Girl** *(Dusie, 2015)… taking Lautréamont's proto-surrealist* **Les Chants de Maldoror** *as inspiration, you imagine the being that results from Maldoror's tumbling sexual tryst with a shark…the consequence being titular 'Tender Girl': an amphibious shark/girl hybrid that arrives on the shores of mankind and spends the novelistic prose-poem's entirety navigating patriarchal and linguistic resistance…exploring, experiencing and encountering…There is so, so much in this book that – before going any further –*

I would like to echo Carol Watts' blurb in seeing the logic of calling it 'a classic for our time' and urge anyone reading this interview, to READ **Tender Girl** *post-haste!*

The interaction between textual and corporeal, somatic and syntactic, drives much of the book…to choose one moment (of many) that switches between a linguistic naming and a physiological functioning:

The body emanates salt perfumes, tiny reeking.
She turns on soft light gets the encyclopedia images and begins
naming her parts: Sisyphus Amanda regicide wisdom serpent clam
pennyroyal bread Roland wingspan commoner fence.

This transitioning back and forth between language and bodily phenomenology often exists in your poetry, I was wondering if you could say a bit about this fascination?

LS

Thank you for your interested words about *Tender Girl*. I feel happy for the intensity of making that book that it can have the kind of committed reading you bring to it. And I think these transitionings you point out are imperative for me; they are the way things are in my experience. I breathe language or am breathed through by language, which yet also morphs in relation to non-lingual feeling and geometric cognizance and diaphanous imbuing. I experience my body intensely and it erupts or soothes itself by way of language. So yes, the transitions go at least "both" ways.

And of course language is its bodies: its sounds, spaces, displacement, stretching letters, ink-shapes, tongues of fire and disdain, clusters of words or letters together (or solo swishes), wishes for ears, electric (digital) trembling, wet electric (mental) happenings, wishes to grow differentials (extensions, new forms) in relation to itself such as with human bodies. So it's volitional, and that wilfulness is part of the social nature of language.

At the same time languages operate always between at least two points or beings, object-events, persons, person-to-text-to-person, so the transitionings you perceive in my writing are always communicative in the broadest sense. Communication as attitude, sense-markers, message transfer, touch, invitation, threat, distance, closeness, and more. And bodies have languages: exhalations and imprecations having to do with blood, marrow, breath, holes, also communication with gestures, expressions, actions, also movement-shapes of the limbs and torso and head: all languages. Every gesture for me is a language in relation with the potentially expressible. So the relation is I suppose dialectical, though I don't know that I have thought of it that way precisely before, much as I live in dialectics.

Are there any writers, films or music that you turn to for inspiration, or in research, when considering the poetics of phenomenology...or for a phenomenology of poetics?

LS

This is an interesting question for me at this point because it shows me that I have not been thinking recently so much about phenomenology per se in terms of reading philosophical works ascribed to it. And yet I think the question is about how I am reading things rather than perhaps what I am reading, thinking of reading as viewing and experiencing also.

In the past I have liked Merleau-Ponty and Michel de Certeau for helping me think about how I encounter thinking and object-events, yet de Certeau wouldn't be considered a phenomenologist. Latterly I have been recurrently obsessed with Charles Sanders Peirce, Theodor Adorno, and Édouard Glissant, whom I am using as support and door-opening thinkers in some as-yet-unpublished essays I am writing. And yet again: not phenomenologists per se, I suppose.

I suspect my more precisely phenomenological ponderings are forwarded by writings that are not disciplinarily philosophical, for example Ida West, a Tasmanian, wrote and published only one book, *Pride Against Prejudice*, which I've also been writing an essay about. The way she uses language as a foreign entity of encounter with the political intensities of her life comes across to me as ethical phenomenology shunted through the challenges of creating any way to speak about life. Leslie Scalapino, too, has long been a phenomenological writer I find really interesting.

As for music: huh. That's such a different realm of being for me from the lingual and the scopic, at least in terms of being a listener. I'm not a devotee of particular musicians nor of type really, unless you want to point to the Unusual, or maybe to "new music" and free jazz and sonic play. I've worked with three composers to make poetry and sound events happen, and I could possibly talk a lot about that, but I want to consider your question in terms of what I "turn to" as a listener. For example in 2016 I encountered the work of trombonist Stuart Dempster, and part of what excited me was the environments – such as the "cistern chapel" (a disused water cistern) he played and recorded in with other musicians – and score-with-open-borders that he seems to work with, at least in terms of how I experience the music. My response to his work is certainly interpretable as devotion to environment and open script within the demands of working one's instruments; that devotion describes at least one part of my phenomenological poetics.

DS

The other most obvious element in **Tender Girl***, which lends it a theoretical urgency, is how, in answering* **Les Chants des Maldoror** *with a hybridised female character – the literally untold story of Maldoror's spawn – you invoke the historically troubled, marginalised, neglected, projected, and falsified presence of women in Surrealist art (I like to think your book belongs to the always more interesting category of 'in dialogue with Surrealism' as opposed to declaratively 'Surrealist'). It also begins to uncover and play with the Surrealism of gendered ex-periences, and presents a shifting female re-configuration of thinking about, and as, Surrealism. Could you say a bit about the interaction between Feminism and Surrealism, as you see it, in* **Tender Girl***?*

LS

Again, I'm so glad you like this book and I am grateful for the book's sake that you have given it so much time. Thank you for that responsive generosity. I know you are interested in Surrealism, which is a set of historical attitudes and procedures I have, at different times, attended to. You doubtless know far more about it than I do at this point, since I moved away from it as a topic of study after graduate school. It's probably true that my moving away was for critical gender reasons, after I shifted from a pretty naïve engagement with Surrealism to a more sceptical one. One might say that working with Laura Riding's writings is the closest I have come to a critical interaction with Surrealism. What I mean is that her writings perform interesting work with surrealism without being particularly astute – or interested in being academically situated in astute dialogue – about Surrealism as a European mode or a set of approaches.

I feel a bit twisted up in answering this question, and I suspect that's because I know how I feel about the question re *Tender Girl*, but I don't know immediately how I think about it. Maybe I'll try to talk about how I feel.

My vision of the inciting idea of the book was sudden and unplanned. I imagined this Girl arising from the sexual encounter between Maldoror and the shark. So the shark gives birth to Girl, and later she rises out of the ocean and I imagined her learning language and learning to interact with the human world. Certainly one can read that sexual encounter in *Les Chants de Maldoror* as a voluntary erotic violence, at least according to the book's language, which is all there is of that imaginary encounter. So the female has already been scarily enstranged in Maldoror's surrealism, which is of course not "surrealism" at all but rather an exuberant-to-violence masculinist imaginary set of encounters that the 20th century French Surrealists took as a grandfather text. This shark cannot speak though she is described as having volition with her body and in her eyeing the human male. And she exists only as language, so in that sense she is "speaking" or being spoken and spoken for.

Yet there's an interesting power balance available in Maldoror's text at that moment, for of course the shark could kill the human easily, is among other sharks doing just that. So their fucking each other is a replacement violent desire. Can we say that imagination is permitted license to think the imagined shark-female has volition in her fucking? Well, the scene is very short, really, so what happens immediately is that we interpret, imagine, prolong or look away from, judge the fantasy that a powerful unlanguaged non-human animal would want to fuck a human. The grounds of Lautréamont's imagining do not have to be ours, yet we are, as readers of the book, meeting his realm. So then, writing out of that realm is re-making the book from that point, empowering an off-script new imagination – or, to think of it in terms of your question, critiquing the book's violence against females, its deployment of imaginative excess in relation to violent permissions.

So the Girl of *Tender Girl* is partly an extra-human avenger – who yet "achieves" nothing in her vengeance. She does not mean to be one, by the way, nor did I plan her that way when writing. She sometimes avenges herself against those who take advantage of her, and she clashes against social pressures; but sometimes she is simply violent accidentally, as part of her physical powers and combinatory body. Almost all the moral action of the book is at least polyvalent, partly because almost all the males of the book are configured as consequences of their worlds. The characters are almost all opaque or symbolic, canvases and response points for the dominant story of Girl.

I think one of the things I have to say in response to this question is that my literate or literary background is itself hybrid. For example I have no grounded relation in a particular discourse of either Surrealism or Feminism. I was carefully trained neither in French Surrealism nor in, say, Continental Feminisms or their Anglo-American-Australasian counterparts or counterpaths. The very name of the principal male in *Tender Girl*, for example, comes from an entirely different place, say a place that is outside of theory unless one zeroes in on the personal in all theory: I chose it because, once upon a time, a kind Palestinian named Ramsey gave me a copy of The Jerusalem Bible, when I was a teenage girl living in Jerusalem. I still have that bible, and the episodic nature of biblical – or, say, recurrent theistic – discourse is part of the self-permission and picaresque of *Tender Girl*. It's like she's a Nothing god-female, an unwitting version of the dual-action divinity in The Book of Job, a litmus slathering through human action. Ramsey is the only male who comes in to any kind of focus and the only character with a normative human name in the book.

So it might be interesting for me to push on why that is, since my carrying on in that fashion was instinctively done rather than critically decided and controlled in terms of how I wrote and revised *Tender Girl*.

Something salvific in the Ramsey character keeps Girl from entirely despising human masculinity, though she still accidentally then increasingly consciously bristles against those male figures who condescend to her and/or molest her. She grows more and more feminist as she has more human experience, and there was never a question that her offspring would be a female, since the offspring is a rebirth of identificatory possibility and a marker of continuation. Also we never know – I never knew – which seed Girl chose from her blue-sharkish pouch for insemination. This matters in terms of your question – which I realize I have veered around in relation to – because volition and plotted blanks, non-available motives and uncharted ingredients, are part of

Girl's powers across the human zones she encounters. Insofar as she is a moving target of para-surrealistic legibility, her character is in type and action evasive of knowing: like history or selves.

One point I think of here, finally, in terms of the Feminism in your question, is that some small part of *Tender Girl* – "part" in the way that a piece of water is part of a large body of water – is a critique of *The Awakening*, a novel I find deplorable, depressing upon the head of woman whilst presented as some kind of female wake-up narrative. In saying all that, it's important to recur to Girl's non-actuality or non-possibility. "Girl" is a nonce equation: biological unachievable, carried by discourse, maybe by theory, which is what your question supposes. I can't answer the matter of feminism and surrealism adequately by resolved exposition nor by normative mimetic dramatic character. So I took it up through Girl.

DS

Building upon the destabilised centrality of bodily experience as textual/textural experience or the relationship between both experiences – a moving back and forth that denies a settling certitude – and considering the title of your collection, **Wild Dialectics** *(Shearsman, 2012), could you elaborate on the role of theory and philosophy in your work? Are you immersed in one and then turn to the other for expression…or are they more simultaneous to you?*

LS

When you write "one" and "the other" in your question, I wonder whether you are contrasting poetry and theory/philosophy, or if you mean theory is one thing and philosophy is "the other"? I prefer to think of the second option because it's so interesting to think about the difference between theory and philosophy.

I have two essay manuscripts developing. Their delay is due to limited time to work, and I admit that my limited writing time gets preferentially allocated to so-called "creative" works, mostly. Anyway the difference between theory and philosophy forms part of the energy in my "creative theory" essay manuscript. That ms. begins with "Wild dialectics," an essay that has nothing to do with my poetry book of that title per se and everything to do with the nominal intuition proposed in my mind by the idea of wild dialectics, which is focused on the hinge of thinking. I realize, though, that I can't really explain that essay nor fully take up your question in the confines of this interview – there's too much to say, and the answer might be: the essays I am writing.

So maybe I'll turn the question a bit: in the way that we say everyone should write poetry, we might say everyone should write theory. Everyone with privilege to think, given basic security and bodily care, should consider how to develop a consciousness rather than assuming they already have one, to paraphrase Nietzsche's critique (in *The Gay Science*). I perceive theory as more open to human permission than philosophy, in terms of its cultural and disciplinary positioning. To be sure, people often try to solidify position and builds walls, but really I think theory is still a free virus among the chances. I reckon perhaps the digitas has opened up those chances in something of the way enjoyed by speculative essays, broadsheets, pamphlets, etc., at various historical periods.

Well, every sentence here is making me think of how much more there is to say, but again I'll curb, and turn to the other interpretation of your question. If I could work on my projects full time I think I would constantly range back and forth between the creative and the critical. As I sometimes say to students, I find each one to be REM sleep for the other. But they are not the same thing to me. I want poetry to be theory; I want creative writing to have the status of first-order thinking. Just because it doesn't, in general, doesn't mean one stops working on that border. When people are irritated by experimental creative work it seems to be because they think creative work should be mimetically normative stories only. Super-short (poems) or extended (narratives), in any event stories.

When people are irritated by experimental theoretical essays, it seems to be at least partly due to a (however understandable) desire for "clear" narrative or for focused furthering of a topic deemed to be disciplinarily shaped. For me, I am not interested in univocal certitude. I'm simply not interested. Nor do I concede any conversations as finished or as dominated by some set of persons or styles. I suppose similar assertions could apply to my poetry, so again: these associated realms of poetry and theory allow my own work to have more discursive instruments and my mind to have more voices.

DS

I'd like to move on to talking about Tomorrowland (Shearsman, 2009), this book-length sequence has led to a film (adaptation/extension) ... in addition to the double CD of accompanying sound experimentation... could you contextualise how this came about? What was your creative relationship like with director Wes Tank?

LS

More big questions!, whose answers encompass years and many possible thoughts. Well, *Tomorrowland* was the first book of mine for which I had the urge to record and compose soundscapes. It's an epic – in the sense of a poem including history, and also in its sustained length – and it's an intensely motivated poem. I wanted a sound performance to exist as an embodied translation of the paper text. There's a narrated quality to the book that comes out probably more vividly in being read aloud. But I also wanted to make soundscapes; I really enjoyed the process of creating sound differentials and thinking about how they could be contra-puntal ambience for the recorded voice of the different sections of the poem. I have many different musical instruments and other sound-making objects and I like to play them dis-connectedly or improperly, to conjure diastolic differentials by way of diachronic systole, to adopt a heart metaphor.

Anyway the film happened very differently and surprisingly: Wes Tank contacted me about making *Tomorrowland* into a film after he had listened to the CDs repeatedly. So I consider that the film started with the CD soundtrack rather than with the paper book. I had known and taught Wes as an undergraduate student in Milwaukee Wisconsin, and he had become in intervening years a musician and videographer in addition to a writer. We met up in person in late 2014 and storyboarded part of the film, which was a fascinating process. Wes printed out the text of "All the Buildings Made of Voices" and cut up the pages into small aspects of lines, 2-6 lines or so apiece, and then glued them to a large board. We went through each of these textual sections and discussed possible interpretations of most of them. What did they mean? How could something like that be filmed?

Finally in June 2016, when I was on research leave and based in Seattle, we filmed with a ten-person crew in Milwaukee. Then in January 2017 Wes flew to New Zealand and we filmed with a more minimal crew. Those two location shoots gave us the footage out of which the *Tomorrowland* film was sculpted and edited. There are countless hours of footage made with multiple cameras, and Wes and his editorial team created what is now the viewable art short. He imagines creating a different and longer version at some point, but whether or not that happens is up in the air. In terms of your question, our working relations have always been great, and it's worth noting that the film result is principally Wes's vision out of the potential of my materials in both the book and the CDs.

DS

You also appear in the film as the alien-like, travelling figure of Eula. Was it important for it be played by you, do you see your poetry in conversation with elements of performance art?

Casting me as Eula was, in the first instance, purely economics. We had no money to make the film, and Wes suggested I play Eula. I had to get over an initial surprise and resistance to the idea. I trusted Wes, so that was not a problem. I just imagined casting someone other than me so I could be more distant from the film, have more of a critical or maker's eye. I also register the fact the film is not the book: Wes has created a film narrative that is not the same thing as the possibilities of *Tomorrowland* as book and as CDs. The film's Eula arrives as a space alien; the book's is not. The film becomes meta-narrative in a way the book really doesn't, for example. But of course a morphic translation – a new mediality – is always different from another media state.

Anyway, I do certainly see my poetry as in conversation with performance art. The CDs are performance art, for example, and I have recorded toward making other CDs that will eventually exist, barring sudden death. I want to make more performances, but again: world enough and time. I have a full-time academic job, and for now performance works happen hither and yon amidst other work.

A different way to take up your question is that the interlacings of signs, the prospects and possibilities of interacting modes, is brought out when something happens with more than one technical aspect or platform of its possibilities. So if there is sound with print, or moving bodies with dialog, then engagement has structured dialectic to work with. When there is modal dialectic, there are multiplied chances to see, feel, and think. Which might seem to put pressure on anything apparently mono-modal. Isn't it okay to read a book, for example? But there again I would say that the reader is the contrapuntal modality: the reader's embodied mind is the performance space of the book's textual object-event. In other words, everything is already multi-modal. Performance art torques and displays and overtly plays the keys of multi-modality.

DS

It also struck me that, in the film, the sense of Eula as a wandering, nomadic explorer …begins to resonate with the character of Girl in **Tender Girl***…is this a consciously reoccurring interest…as the outsider, a female (but whose gender seems ambiguously in play away from any binary) who allows a perspective through which to re-encounter everyday experience…to estrange and interrogate our accepted experiences? It reminded me, to an extent, of Scarlett Johansson's alien abductress in Jonathan Glazer's adaptation of Michel Faber's novel Under the Skin (2013).*

LS

I have not seen that Glazer film. But I can say that once I realized what Wes Tank wanted to do with Eula, I thought of *Liquid Sky*, the Slava Tsukerman film from the 1970s that made a keen impression on me when I saw it on video in the 1990s. If you have seen that Tsukerman film then you can imagine how Eula became a visualization for me in terms of Wes's film vision. In terms of picaresque experiences, though, Girl is much more akin to the *Liquid Sky* heroine than Eula is, in both the book and the film version of *Tomorrowland*. Oh, things get all interwrapt!

Certainly a predominantly female-figured consciousness in imagined cultural spaces has become a legible obsession in my works. Hardly surprising, perhaps. I am more interested in the differentiations in various works than in the type-trace per se. But it's possibly interesting to see this androgynous-female figuration intensify in my work. In the *Tomorrowland* book Eula isn't a character so much as a para-narratorial figuration whose name stands for End User License Agreement and whose position is partly androgynous contemporary. Similarly but not identically, the other named principles of the book are not characters but symbolic forces. But Wes had to, or wanted to, work with human actors, and he set up Eula in a fairly stable body relation to actors who play the other named principles (ideas, that is, not mains) in the *Tomorrowland* book, that is: Fasti, Manda, and Jack.

DS

What films have inspired you in the past?

LS

I suppose it's worth mentioning that I wasn't raised with films. I saw possibly ten films in cinemas before the age of about 14, and after that I went only somewhat more often until I got into my 30s. I don't consider that I have much sophistication or depth of knowledge about film, though in the last decade I've seen a lot of children's films because of raising my son and mostly watching movies that appeal to children.

Most of the time I don't want to see what is showing at the cinemas because it sounds too obvious: pre-interpreted dramatic situations of greater or lesser intensity. However, there are films that have moved me a great deal, and of course film as a medium has formidable powers of engagement with our bodily (scopic, sonic, and kinetic) and leisure-motivated (cinema-going) and critical selves. I've just mentioned the Tsukerman film. If I had my way I would almost always watch strange films, things like Buñuel's, anime whose resolution isn't too loud – perhaps *The Red Turtle* is a good contemporary example, mytho-symbolic as it is, though I saw *Spirited Away* when it first came out in theatres and I can't think of an anime film I like better.

I should try to answer your question with more specifics. What films have inspired me? With manipulated dread and nausea: *Pan's Labyrinth*, and its type of film. With desire and curiosity,

Orphée. With discomfited interest, Theresa Hak Kying Cha's short films, and similar short works whose makers and titles I forget because I have simply come across them while scrolling through ubuweb looking for moving image work. Werner Herzog's films, too, especially *Fitzcarraldo*. Oh and also the legible-as-film digital kinetics of some of the work in the online Electronic Literature Collections, the most effective collocation of digital/new media works that I know of at present, however one might think at least twice about the ELC's English-dominant orientations.

DS

The merging of film and poetry, or the one-in-the-other dynamic, is a really difficult, but fascinating area – are there any particular coordinates of film or poetry that you look to as encapsulations of when these two mediums work well together?

LS

This is a good question. The problem of language in relation to anything else rises up acutely. The potential swamping of abstraction by sensory particulars also. I've already talked about multi-modality, so I think here I'll say something about control and the open line. I have an essay called "Soft text and the open line" (coming out in Axon journal), and I'm thinking of it now because I know part of my experienced resistance to watching films is about control and swamping. Except when I go to the movies for what I call brain candy films, I don't want to be seized by art; I want to be conscious. To sustain that consciousness, I want art to leave openings in itself. Such openings might be what are sometimes judged to be mistakes, which I think is part of the public pleasure in continuity errors in film editing – modern watches on the wrists of historical characters, for example, allow or force the audience to become conscious of the made experience. That consciousness actually increases the pleasure of immersion in the constructed film, at least for some viewers.

But open lines can happen in more deliberately constructed ways: internally-skewed aspects of a work can function as waking points, breath moments interposing in the coherence of a made work. These open moments can be rougher, and perhaps feel like mistakes, or somewhat smoother and structured into a non-integrated and yet whole work.

Even in terms of open lines film and poetry have different "coordinates," as you are calling them here. For the sake of considering this question further, I want to acknowledge yet set aside the expansive possibilities for "film" and "poetry," either of which can be almost anything that a maker and context wish to say they are. So film could be, for example, an audience raising its mobile phones – in a theatre with no central film showing – and filming what they see for ten minutes, then declaring the end of "the film." Or poetry could be a person being handed slips of language written on tree leaves by another person right then on a boat, reading the slips aloud, then letting them fly out to sea.

Actually, though I intended to imagine two examples that are different from a film in a cinema and a poem on a page being read in a book or on a screen, I find those imagined examples of ephemerally-focused control-loosening film and poetry to provide sufficient images of modal "coordinates." The scopic-experience orientation of the filmic and the performed-interpretation orientation of poetry have a great deal to offer each other in terms of exponentializing dialectic opportunities and therefore mental food.

DS

You have mentioned in another interview (on 'Jack Ross: Opinions') the writers you are most often drawn to: 'certain writers are recurrent for me, sometimes as a matter of the note I need to have plucked at a moment of thinking. Writers of excess can help me re-imagine our boundaries and exposures in the world – here I'm thinking of William Blake, Lautréamont, Friedrich Nietzsche, Laura Riding, Georges Bataille, Kathy Acker, William Vollmann.' I was wondering whether the world-creating and ambitious excess of these writers, which certainly enters your work in the book-length explorations of **Tomorrowland, Gender City, Tender Girl,** *and* **Symphony for Human Transport,** *is something that you think any other contemporary poets are doing? Who have you read recently that excites you?*

It isn't poetry, but I read without stopping *The Stolen Island* (2017), Scott Hamilton's narrative of the pillaged island of 'Ata. It speaks within alternative histories of places – and I mean alternative ways of telling and considering histories – with and from a sustained "irrational" commitment (the way love is an irrational commitment) to Oceania ethics, identity, and histories. And Erín Moure's *Kapusta* (2015) is one of my favourite recent books: translingual poetry and prose, experimental drama, investigation of communal and familial self – it performs multiply. Alice Notley's poetry books are go-to readings for stripped encounter, not to be reductive, but certainly to be summary in terms of your question. By stripped encounter I suppose I mean poetry written in an unvarnished (hence "stripped") self-encountering with many different aspects of life and death and utter commitment to imagination as thinking bodies. These encounters are of course artistically considered and shaped, and I'm conscious of imagining how they were written when I am reading her books.

In terms of "world-creating and ambitious excess," well, people create in their contexts and therefore zeitgeist recurrences zoom out everywhere. I am sure there are many poets writing now, whether or not I am aware of them, whose work features this large-creating aspect of imagining that you reference in your question. Don Mee Choi, for example, has completely entered my zones of attention: I am moved and discomfited by everything she writes, and she too writes in multi-modal history and lingual re-making. And in terms of more writing I am excited by – it's hard to pause and think of more writers to mention, but some come up without too much push: Laressa Dickey and Nathanaël, for example, are both in the new *women : poetry : migration* (2017), edited by Jane Joritz-Nakagawa, who has performed a service for the transnational imaginaries I live in by compiling this anthology. And the writers included in my own anthology *A TransPacific Poetics* (2017, co-edited with Sawako Nakayasu) are resonantly interesting for me: Don Mee is there, and Melanie Rands and Jai Arun Ravine for example. And in the new Chicago Review issue, Anne Kawala is a discovery for me; I'd like to find more of her poetry to read.

[2018]

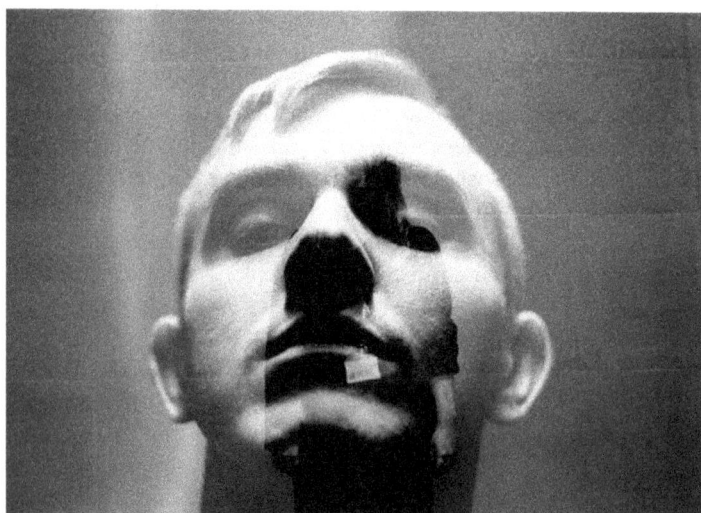

S J F O W L E R

It seems logical that SJ Fowler's poetry would find itself in, and as, film...at some point. Steve's poetry has taken his roving attention into performance art and sound art; into and through elements of comedy and theatre; from concrete poetry and the sculptural towards the pictorial, chance-led, accidental, and ritualistic; and in acts of art / poetry (the slash ever present) that move hungrily out of discipline and into abandon...why would the filmic not be there? Fluttering or strobing, as a kind of inevitable encounter, film, and the intensity of its absorptive hold, seems a natural partner (sparring and / or dancing, fighting and / or loving) for a poet so inventively conscious of how a performance can befriend, baffle or challenge an audience. In his KFS collection from 2011, *Red Museum*, the first poem begins:

> & the doors of a second way
> open to a third light
> which was dark

To start in the conjunctive ampersand, we begin as movement that has gone before beginning and, and only as or in that and, into 'the doors of a second way'. The poem invites a quick push into revolving thresholds 'open to a third light', and we enter Fowler's breathless space (the descent, in this book, into the burbling entrails of the British Museum) in order to open up, if only opening again and again, meeting the 'light/which was dark'. The poetry is a contested, revolving, and pluralised movement... what better way to greet the possibility of film in poetry?

DS

On the evening of curated film and poetry as part of your Mahu Exhibition in 2015, I remember you were particularly pleased to see a still from Bergman's **Persona** *(1966) in my presentation....and I think, though I might have misremembered this, that it was primarily his industrious and prolific output that you admired?*

That was a lovely evening but I do remember feeling guilty at how small the venue was when I saw your face melt a wee bit. On Bergman, I think so, though perhaps not primarily what I admire about him. I think I mentioned to you that I grew up really with no literature or art of any designated kind in my household (there was lots of creativity, for want of a better word, but nothing people would think of as art) and it was film (through a sky TV subscription and the Film4 channel) that was my first ever introduction to that which might be called complex creative works.

What I noticed then, and was confused by, was that filmmakers, and this is obviously true of authors and all artists, become known for single works often, and people talk about their output, their whole life of work, through the lens of a single work. Which seems unfair. With Bergman, it was the first time I did a deep dive on someone's work. I watched dozens of his films. I was 15 maybe. It just got into me that is what you do. You take a subject or idea you are fascinated by, you find the right method to reveal it and you go about that, back to back, year on year. You let the audience follow you, you don't follow them. And my family is very working class and my parents old, and they were all about work ethic.

DS

Since 2011 you have written 7 collections, 4 art books, 7 collaborative collections, a feature film, a book of essays, exhibited at galleries across Europe, taught widely, and continue tirelessly to organise a staggering number of events involving poets across Europe and the UK. Is the prolific nature of your art something you have always aimed for – is it an ambitious work ethic or a compulsive necessity?

SJF

I've thought about this, tried to think through whether I am compelled, and question myself first. I have regular moments of pretty severe doubt, thinking my work to be meaningless. It is pretty much useless. And I understand completely I drown my own reception through volume. But I am increasingly sure it's an expression of something crucial to me. My mind, my body, it moves at pace, I really enjoy prolificism, and admire it in others. I don't know why it appears unusual? I think, sometimes, people in poetry have a vision of reception that I don't understand. This is the break. They are always imagining their readers, and in so doing, they are trying to change or affect them. This is so essential to our artistic culture that no one thinks about it sometimes. But I have no desire to alter another human being through my work. That seems presumptive, if not inherently righteous, if not mad, if not ignoring the nature of other minds. I also think there's a paradox at play. The less you try to change people through your work, the more likely you are to do so. I don't affect many with what I do, small numbers, but those who respond to my stuff seem to really respond.

Essentially, I create works for my own contentedness. For myself. And I work hard, because it brings me pleasure. I don't work as hard as I did when I did real jobs. I don't work as hard as most humans on this planet. I just put in hours of work every day, at everything I like to do. This tends to produce lots of stuff and makes me happy enough. There is almost nothing in my life that I do that I don't choose to do.

DS

And besides Bergman, who are the poets / artists / film-makers you look to as models for this ambitious rate of production?

SJF

I think with the way I see my work, using poetry as a means of intervention into the language of the world as I find it, as it occurs in my head and out of my mouth, as an artform referent to language whose primary aim is not necessary communication or information but maybe reflection or repositioning for those willing to give attention enough to notice that, it makes sense that my influences aren't poets, primarily. I mean I've said this in loads of conversations and so many poets seem relieved and say the same.

Also, I consume a lot of different and weird stuff. So I'd say huge influences on me in terms of work and being prolific

129

would be people like Chris Morris, Harry Nilsson, Peter Greenaway, Harold Pinter, Tom Raworth, Maja Jantar, Yoram Kaniuk, Alejandra Pizarnik, Josh Homme, Ghedalia Tazartes, Peter Weiss, Henri Michaux, Asger Jorn. There's loads. They all worked hard. It's pretty normal for artists to be industrious in certain creative fields. It's not unusual to generate lots of material outside of poetry.

DS

You and Joshua Alexander's first feature length film, **Animal Drums***, premiered at Whitechapel Gallery on December 13th 2018... beyond any distinction between video-art, avant-garde film and narrative cinema, it was instead a kind of city-as-psyche-as-performance-docu-art-haemorrhage-state-of-the-aberration-that-is-London kind of a deal...had you always wanted to make a feature film and do you and Joshua want to make more?*

SJF

I never wanted to make a film as I didn't want to direct, as that's very much my personality type and I've spent my adult life avoiding positions like that in order to be calmer, without stress, antagonism and so I need not make the sacrifices one has to make to make a film. *Animal Drums* grew out of circumstance – my friendship with Josh, who is remarkably talented and unusually resourceful, and how we met, working at the British Museum. It grew into a feature after years of meeting, filming, playing with ideas. It became itself over time, and then inevitably captured how the city was changing around us.

DS

How did the process of making a film influence your poetic practice or do you see them both as porously part of the same project?

SJF

I don't know what my poetic practice is, as it changes from book to book, idea to idea, commission to commission, collaboration to collaboration. I don't have a singular project or vision either, just hoping for interesting things to fill my days before I go. The film initially relied on my poetry to drive it, often with voice overs. I was confident working with language this way into film, the interesting part was trying to successfully marry that with the potentials of cinematic grammar.

DS

During the making of the film were there any filmmakers that were instructive points of reference for either you or Joshua?

SJF

For me Gaspar Noe, Peter Greenaway, Cristi Puiu. For Josh, very different folk I think.

DS

As the film features Iain Sinclair and is certainly in a dialogue (literally at one point) with Sinclair's interests, I wondered whether the films of Andrew Kötting were significant – as not only does he frequently collaborate with Sinclair and Alan Moore (whose voice is alarmingly similar to a lot of the pitch-shifted voiceover in **Animal Drums***) but his 'feet-on-the-ground' bustling of performance and physicality seem close to much of your praxis….*

SJF

I think so. I saw *This Filthy Earth* when it came out, I was at university and my best friend was from Kendall in Cumbria and he hated it. I felt the opposite. When I started writing, Iain Sinclair was someone I met after maybe six months. I walked up to him after a lecture and he really helped me, he's remarkably generous like that. He introduced Kötting's work to me anew and it must've been there in my mind, conceptualising *Animal Drums.*

DS

Now, here, at the half-way point, let's move from Drums to Devils: your latest collection, **I stand alone by the Devils (Broken Sleep Books)**, *and other poems on films, gathers together a selection of poems that are all directed from, or to, specific films. Firstly, I wanted to ask whether this idea had been around for a while or whether there was something in particular that recently (the completion of* **Animal Drums***?) inspired this explicit tribute to cinema?*

SJF

The collection has been around for years. This happens with a lot of my books; they begin with a single work, grow slowly and an unforeseen event speeds them into being. The unforeseen event in this case was not the Drums but a sudden spate of watching and rewatching films. I just feel back into it, regained the patience one needs. For the first time, I remembered when I was a teenager, a bit lonely, watching like five art films a day for two years. I had never once thought this might've been an influence on what I do now, for a living. Which seems stupid now.

DS

Many of the directors you include (Ken Russell, Werner Herzog, David Cronenberg, Nicolas Roeg, Gasper Noe, Lars Von Trier,) and many of the films (Pasolini's **Salo***, Vinterberg's* **Festen***, Zulawski's* **Possession***) are known for their extremity, shock, or supposedly transgressive nature. It seems clear to me that being drawn towards the challenge of discomfort and our own interpretations of threat and vulnerability are elements that needle through much of your poetry. Did these films help inspire those interests in your poetic practice, or was it more a case of them resonating with a pre-existing sense that art should advance into a troubled / troubling space in order to better question itself and the viewer/ reader?*

SJF

It's funny, while I do recognise these films are intense, I haven't conceived them that way. It's just what I'm interested in, that serious investment of attention should be met with challenge and complexity. I'd say your question is interesting because you didn't mention that most of the films are European, especially the 'violent' ones. In European cinema, and European culture in general, it seems obvious that art must reveal the most awful truth of human behaviours, because they are true, through fictional means. This is difficult to experience, but not unpleasant. I know some people seem to think fictional violence is worse than the real thing happening on their street but it's just my taste that films and art, that are serious, not intending to give you a nice brain fog, which has its place, should not comfort and reassure. So, I'd move the terms of the question and say these films aren't about violence but culture.

DS

Could you say a bit about the process of writing these poems?

SJF

There are multiple methods at play but quite a few involved note taking, of dialogue, of scene description, of ideas happening in language while I was watching. So they are found poems in a sense, then blended through edits and additions. Translations in a weird sense, as much as responses. Others were written from memories of the films, what they come to represent for me, idiosyncratically. Others from research, post-watching, digging through books about the films or their makers. I saw myself as only trying to be faithful to each specific piece of cinema, and doing so by choosing not only the language of the poem and its machinery, but also the method of that.

DS

Some of the films you have chosen adopt incredibly stylised palettes for their communication, prioritising and innovating aesthetics as ways to newly become or imagine their content...I'm thinking of the baroque geometry of Derek Jarman's sets for Russell's **The Devils** *or the possessed melodrama of the performances; the theatrical flamboyance of Peter Greenaway's horror; the icy fits of anguish as chore-ography, or domestic collapse as tentacular tryst in Zulawski's* **Possession;** *or the radical Dogme approach of early Von Trier and Vinterberg...did these stylistic elements propel a desire for your poetry to stretch its form or 'style' and whatever that might encompass ?*

SJF

That's very possible. Though I do think this enjoyment of film I had was extremely genuine and remains so, in that I don't notice any of the techniques or aesthetics while watching in a knowing or mindful way. Of course I see them, but for example I cannot read an interesting book of any kind now without taking copious notes, and I don't ever finish some books because they are too intimidatingly full of material that I feel I need to steal or respond to. Books are joyful work to me, resources for my own things. Films I am passive to, as most people are. But they must have affected me early on. Maybe Peter Greenaway is the exception here, because his films feel very literally poetic.

DS

Another recurrent theme, in the chosen films as in much of your poetry (in this collection and elsewhere) is the prickling shifts, artifice, behaviours and psychology of masculinity. There seems to often be – in your poetry as in these films – the presentation (or exploration) of masculinity as a bullying challenge of violence, muscled out as a language or code that is always inseparable from intimacies of its fear and vulnerability. I think your poetry very often drives at this uncomfortable and violent slippage, between a boasting threat and anxiety, often asserted in spelling changes that dare the reader to label them as errors, along with calculated accidents, contractions and line breaks...could you maybe say a bit about how the performances of masculinity animate these poems, and the performances of literary/literacy as its own code to break and re-make in your po-ems...and how this connects to your relationship with these films?

I don't know. I'm not sure I know what masculinity means in this, or other aesthetic contexts (it gets brought up a lot to me), as I think I try to resist the formulations of these ideas made by people who want to systemise them for PhD's and things like that. I will say simply that I did not choose to come from a working-class background and an intense masculine environment and I have done my utmost to live my life with as much kindness and gentleness as possible. Despite this I can't void myself of what feels like a necessary engagement with these themes or ideas. I, more than most, wish to mock masculine pretentions because I was horrified and confronted by them as a child, young adult, working as a doorman and when I did martial arts for money. I've been in some incredibly intense environments that were male dominated. But there is obviously virtue in these cultures and environments too, qualities that do not exist in the bourgeois world I currently inhabit. This is often revealed in the cinema I'm drawn to, in the way they are made as well as the content of the films. Galoup in *Beau Travail*, Urban Grandier in *The Devils* (Oliver Reed in general), Harry Angel in *Angel Heart*, Tomek in *A Short Film About Love*. Etc... These films are often far more ambiguous, critical and subversive about these issues than people think and I want my poetry to be like that too.

DS

Are you most interested in art (poetry / film) when it seems to challenge the audience or perhaps dares the audience into challenging themselves?

SJF

A quote I came across recently. *If you try to please audiences, uncritically accepting their tastes, it can only mean that you have no respect for them.* Andrei Tarkovsky. It can't be said better.

DS

Many of your poems manage to probe and inhabit the blunt or damaging aspects of how cruel or upsetting language can become and how controversy can spark productive, if uncomfortable, discussion, as part of a progressive element of cultural/societal interrogation. I'm thinking about the voices collected in **Minimum Security Prison Dentistry** *(2011), the darkness of Disney as a mutilated puppetry of sexuality and gender in* **House of Mouse** *— your fantastic collaboration with Prudence Chamberlain (KFS, 2017) — or the labyrinth of barbarism in* **Red Museum** *(KFS, 2011). These all explore morality, as many of the films in this latest collection, without ever offering explicit reassurance. I was wondering whether you might be able to talk this through...*

SJF

I am really fascinated with how poetry seems to not view itself as the medium in which we might explore what language is doing now, in the 21st century, as well as (or instead of) the vehicle of particular opinion and self-expression. Often, at the moment, it seems to be about reattaching a power to language that is subjective at the expense of a fundamental concern about exploring what the context is around language itself. Maybe an intellectual, thick skinned literature that explores how we might be giving power away to people who aren't very clever by taking meaning from words that are something other than they appear might be a good thing.

Minimum Security, for example, is often made up of prison slang or phraseology, that I wrote down way before I got into poetry, and didn't really know what poetry was, when I very briefly worked in a prison. It scared me, the prison, it messed me up, giving me nightmares for years. It was a maximum-security prison. I found the notebook years later, when writing and realised I must've somehow written this stuff down as an outlet. I turned that into poetry, often as it was found, often written through (in two weeks, thanks to the invitation to publish from Colin Herd). I mention this just to offer context as to why I often experience moments of fissure between how I perceive language, morality, poetry, and how I'm told others do.

Your earlier poetry found an affinity with (and endorsement from) the restless cut and wit of Tom Raworth, and the punk humour and occultist parodies of Stewart Home (who appears in **Animal Drums***). Are there any contemporary poets in the UK that you feel similarly attuned to, or that you look to for inspiration? I ask this as I feel that your poetry often feels quite outside of, or apart from, the most visible or familiar UK trends and traditions – which I find interesting for a poet who has done so much to tirelessly bring UK poets together.*

Definitely a big compliment, thank you. There is absolutely loads of people working now whom I think are remarkable. I often am motivated to put on events to watch them, and often think what I see in people's work, away from a fundamental sensitivity to what appears authentic (whatever that means), is that I want to steal from them. In this way, they are different than this tradition I'm interested in, and it's because they are proper different than me that I like them. There's a lot more people working in Europe with whom I have a very close sensibility, like Max Hofler, Maja Jantar, Robert Prosser, Fabian Faltin and loads of others.

And, as an enjoyably unimaginative concluding question: what was the last film you really enjoyed?

Though my poems on films book is finished I am still deep in the watching mode. I watched *Alice Doesn't Live Here Anymore* (dir. Martin Scorsese, 1974) and *Barton Fink* (dir. Coen Brothers, 1991) over the last few days. Both brilliant, as good as I remembered from 20 years ago.

[2019]

*I*A*I*N *S*I*N*C*L*A*I*R*

In his introduction to *The Firewall: Selected Poems 1979 – 2006* (etruscan books, 2006), Iain Sinclair reflects, '[t]hey were the double lives I wanted most, film and poetry'. From his first book of poems (*Back Garden Poems*, 1970) and first film (*Ah Sunflower!*, 1967) onwards, Sinclair's prolific and inventive work has travelled between those 'double lives' with such energy that doubles double: film, poetry, prose, documentary, memoir, history, place and the occultist exploration and collapse of all in restless combination have built a unique territory.

His own body of work a seething accretion of place, open to the same psychogeographic readings he pioneered. Following the novel, *Downriver* (1991), winner of the James Tait Black Memorial Award, many readers know Sinclair through the connotations of Psychogeography. The writer as walker, perambulating London's hallucinatory archaeologies of time through literary esoterica, off-the-radar experimentations, the grisly interventions of history, and the 'reforgotten' luminaries constellating nomads of the British underground.

And yet, what a gulf between that energy and the emptied 'brand' of 'Psychogeography' as it is most commonly perceived and practiced now. Encompassing histories of art, activism, literature and philosophy from Baudelaire and Guy Debord, what Sinclair sparked with new momentum began in the searing diary conspiracies of two long experimental poems from the 70s, *Lud Heat* and *Suicide Bridge*. Crackling ley lines between American and British poetry, drawing Blake and London graveyards into the paranoid revelations of Burroughs and the Projective breath of Black Mountain School poetics, specifically Charles Olson and Ed Dorn. Sinclair continued this contagious spirit across film (collaborating with Chris Petit, John Rogers, Grant Gee and Andrew Kötting) and in the ranging documentary prose of his London books. Now, far from the original circles of 60s and 70s avant-garde writing, or meandering in the unique atmosphere of W.G. Sebald, those connections between Sinclair, Rachel Lichten-stein, Alan Moore, Gareth Evans, Stephen Watts, Patrick Keiller, Brian Catling, and Stewart Home, have left 'Psychogeography' as it becomes an increasingly hollowed tribute to its previous energy. Now more commonly encountered in the plodding reverence for the word 'liminal' and insipid academic riffs than ever actually building upon Sinclair's work and its restless eye. A writer that merged inspiration from the dazzling rubble of Stan Brackhage's films with the quick-cut observation of Tom Raworth's poetry, is not likely to stand still. The writer, as the writing, is always journeying. The language and the light is moving.

My reading of Sinclair has always been – in all my self-absorbed insecurity – refracted through negotiating a desire to write that is (inevitably?) estranged from the hierarchies of awards culture, big publishers and the immediacy of social media. Reading Sinclair conferred a sense of permission and empowered assurance, to connect with a British history of writers that flourished far from such platforms (and before such platforms existed). To find an alternative map. The rites of lost paths and buried signs.

Whilst teaching Creative Writing on and off for a few years, I was always concerned with how much the university department pedalled awards culture. On one hand, I once taught a module on Critical Theory and Awards Culture…and on the other, the department's hiring and structure was governed by the very same power dynamic of cultural capital it alleged to dismantle. Deconstruct all but the methods of deconstruction. But that is a very academic hypocrisy, prevalent in English and Creative Writing departments; constantly perpetuating the markets of evaluation that their staff and students have learnt to critique. An institution predicated on the same economies of value it purports to resist, leading to the cognitive dissonance of academic employment: advocating that which you will never embody. Meanwhile, outside of the 'Art of the Proposal' (Sinclair's phrase), the bureaucratized judgements of validity, impositions of business models and palliative responsibility, in addition to the advertising frenzy of social media, there are ways of living and writing that connect – as they always have and always will – beyond these contradictions of 'success'.

This context clearly led my own approach to Sinclair and formulated its own preconceived map of where the interview 'might go' – a devised narrative which Sinclair observes in his first answer. His writing is peopled by the writers that mainstream literary success will never anoint with that noxious perfume, prestige; those in their contemporaneity that will rarely find external affirmation but constitute, in correspondence, a strength and progress that transcends aspirations for recognition to instead exist in the conviction of its creation. The film with less backing has more freedom, the smaller press can take bigger risks. It is not re-configuring an embittered response to neglect or small readership like some unconvincing and masochistic integrity of elected obscurity. But instead, it is exploring the fervent turbines of art that carry on regardless, or that pitch themselves so far into the future or entangled so thoroughly in the past that their reception in the present will always be troubled. Admirably mad ambition thrives in the dark; modest pot-plants become ravenous triffids and ideas escalate into their own ragged jungles. It is the strange and committed play of the imagination and not its advertised image. The unpredictable tangent and not the promise of yet another application form. The weird, divisive and unfinished, not the by-committee labelling of merit. Vision before image.

Allen Ginsberg facing Sinclair's camera in 1967, speaks directly into the lens:

> If you will keep your mind on the image in front of you...which is my face in the camera or in your TV tube, or screen, and realise that I'm looking too – into a little black hole, imagining that you are there, and also imagining what would be possible to say that would actually communicate through all the electricity and all the glass and all the dots on the electric screen – so you're not deceived by the image seen but that we are all on the same beam, which is you're sitting in your room, surrounded by your body, looking at a screen, and I'm sitting in my garden, with my body, with the noise of cars outside – so we're at least conscious of where we are and don't get hypnotized into some false universe of pure imagery.

And then, 60 years later, in a documentary about *The Last London*, Sinclair is looking around at signs and adverts, posters, paint, digital promises of property development, and imagined virtual utopias, he observes that the city is

> cannibalised in imagery – a monster eating itself with images of images of images – all the way through until we disappear into a great white dot.

I'd like to start by returning: to your occult diary as prose poetry... or prose as poetry and the emergence of poetry's ley lines between: **Lud Heat** *(Albion Village Press, 1975). Part feverish detective dream and part architectural autopsy, it threads and frays its searching eye through Ancient Egypt and the Ancient Greek histories of Herodotus and onwards through to Milton, Thomas De Quincey, Blake, Rimbaud, Yeats, Eliot, Pound, Olson, and further out spinning into the (then) present of Brian Catling, Chris Torrence and other counter-culture poetics of the 60s and 70s (a hieratic resonance with Lee Harwood's* **The Long Black Veil***, 1970-72, and the London traversals of Allen Fisher's* **PLACE***)...it is a long poem that, in short, draws together propulsive vision through a subterranean trail of poetic and literary coordinates...and yet also, running throughout is the presence of Film. There are references to F.W. Murnau, John Wayne, Bergman, Hammer Horror, Hollywood, Mario Bava, and Nicolas Roeg's* **Performance***...and the filmmaker that most explicitly overlooks the poetic/cinematic axis of the poem's heat and dig – giant of the American avant garde – Stan Brackhage.His film,* **TheActofSeeingWithOne'sOwnEyes***, and his essay 'margin alien' both connect and surface in* **Lud Heat***... I was wondering whether you could talk a bit about his influence in your work? It seems there is a really comparable energy in the restless and associative nature of his films and your writing (in prose and poetry) – where a Blakean vision meets the observational diary form. As well as his influence in your work, could you maybe also say a bit about your first experiences of encountering Brackhage's films?*

My problem with the necessary distance of this quarantine interrogation is that the questions you put are confessing, at length, whatever you found useful in reading my early books - while formulating your own counter-narrative through a lively and engaged critique. There really is no requirement for me to add anything further. I've had my say, back then, and a forced return to the territory is, inevitably, unreliable and self-serving. If we were sitting together, taking our time, or even in a seminar room, there would be space for useful digression and gossip, new detours and weirder improvisations. To keep it alive. It's like ranting down a dead telephone, instead of muttering at a human in a chair.

As always – as I have found in shaping interviews for books that I have published – the editor, however pure his intentions, dominates the angle of the response. Your take, here, is the real work. Asking is composing. Like any politician, it is too easy to supply the answers we want to give, disregarding the barbs in the question.

On *Lud Heat*, taking off from your generous evaluation, the question emerges of Brakhage's influence on my work. And my answer, such as it is, in trying to recollect the temperature of that moment, when the impetus was still raw, is plainly there in the book: the section inspired by a Brakhage film: '*Rites of Autopsy, The Act of Seeing With One's Own Eyes...* viewed June 10, 1974.' Autopsies of various sorts, cultural, topographic, literal, are the theme of that book. And Brakhage's steady gaze was a model to which I aspired.

In my copy of Brakhage's little black publication, *A Moving Picture Giving and Taking Book*, I have a postcard from the man. It says one word: 'Blessings'. A benediction I was delighted to receive. It was good to know that Brakhage had seen, and was not alarmed by, my effusion. My speculative response to his autopsy film was one of those things that arrived when it was most needed, and it came fast, with little or no revision, according with laws of composition framed by Jack Kerouac. The book was acquired in Compendium, Camden Town: 8 November 1972. One of the co-dedicatees is Michael McClure. I was fascinated to hear the West Coast poet's reminiscences of Brakhage when I visited him. An episode touched on in *American Smoke*.

The film visionary also collaborated with Ed Dorn, one of the major inspirations at the time of *Lud Heat* and *Suicide Bridge*. The Howard Hughes piece in Suicide Bridge came directly out of Gunslinger. The back-story of *Abilene! Abilene!*, the Western script Dorn wrote at Brakhage's invitation, has now been published by The Center for the Humanities, The City University of New York. And is well worth checking out. Dorn's delighted ruminations on the cultural (and economic) consequences of cattle drives find their way, old influences coming full circle now, into the book I am presently labouring on, *The Gold Machine*.

Perhaps, at this stage, taking a breath, I should pay particular attention to how Brakhage concludes his book?

Until that maker himself becomes too long exposed to the light of any particular piece of film and, thus, ceases to see it any longer... then, and then only, might a work be called 'finished'.

It was always about light, light and heat. And browsing, scavenging, cannibalising all available energy sources. In 1963 I got my hands on a copy of *Film Culture* (*Special Issue: American Directors, Part 2*), edited by Jonas Mekas. McClure was writing about Brakhage's *Dog Star Man* as 'the first 16mm epic'. I was interested in the idea of 'open field' composition – splicing prose, poetry, image, documentation, polemic, genre – into a version of the epic, specifically on a patch of London ground. Brakhage's association with McClure and the Black Mountain poets was the vital link between the two areas in which I wanted to operate: film and poetry. The silence of his films (as with the films of Maya Deren) was another attraction. But, in this case, the reading came first: letters, fragments of scripts and comments of other filmmakers.

By the mid-sixties, I was catching up with the films themselves. And, fired by what we had seen (as well as by the Mekas notion of a film 'Diary' recording accidents of everyday life), I became part of a Hackney group keeping a community 8mm film record, quite intensely, from about 1969 to 1975 (the date of publication of *Lud Heat*). Some of the films were records of place and activity (using single-frame click-click for reasons of economy) and some were Brakhage-permitted 'Songs' (using multiple superimpositions). Elements spilled into the self-published books of that period.

When, on a unique visit to my house, I showed some of these films to Jeremy Prynne, he revealed that he not only knew the work of Brakhage (not surprising, given his nexus of transatlantic friends and correspondents), but had visited him. That was one of the great excitements of the era, how, quite suddenly, everything folded in on itself. And the possibilities seemed infinite.

DS

Following on from, and not unrelated to, Brackhage – I was really interested in asking you a bit about your reading of Robert Duncan at that time. I feel that, unlike Burroughs, the Beats or

Charles Olson, Duncan is not as frequently mentioned in relation to your poetry – despite **Suicide Bridge** *(Albion Village Press, 1979) starting with an epigraph from Duncan's mytho-poetic monolith of musings,* **The H.D. Book** *(composed between 1959 and 1964). Were you interested in the artistic links between him and Kenneth Anger's films? Did you draw any inspiration from the collage art of Duncan's partner, Jess? How often do you find yourself returning to American poets of this era?*

IS

At that time, I read promiscuously, going back to Yeats (who is also quoted in *Lud Heat*). I'd drawn on the Byzantium poems and other things when I lived in London in 1962, but pulled back when I was in Dublin as a student. He was too loud and too much approved and promoted as a presence in that city. But I picked up on *A Vision*, alongside serious sampling in Duncan. My Duncan engagement was never as intense as the ongoing binges around Olson, but I continued to dip and snack, zooming in on those aspects you mention, the 'mytho-poetic monolith of musings'. Eric Mottram often spoke about the audiences Duncan offered, great free-flowing monologues, at his house in Herne Hill. 'That's Duncan's chair!' he announced as the photographer Marc Atkins was about to settle himself in the wrong place.

I knew a little about the links with Anger. (I shared a Chinese meal with him once in Newcastle.) But I didn't, back then, make any particular connection with the collage art of Jess. I had the vague and probably unfounded prejudice that there was something enclosed, too hermetic and strategically interior in that scene. But aspects of Duncan's vaulting ambition and truth-to-vocation were always attractive. The Fulcrum books were usually somewhere at hand.

DS

With your editing of the poetry anthology, **Conductors of Chaos** *(1966), you brought together poets associated with the 'British Poetry Revival' as well as an alternative ancestry of British Modernism and Surrealism that included – for example – Nicholas Moore and David Gascoyne. From that period, drawing from Eric Mottram and Bob Cobbing and the activities around* *bookshops like Better Books, I was wondering how much notable interaction was going on between poets and film-makers? The relationship between poets and filmmakers in the American avant-garde (from Alfred Lesli and Frank O'Hara, Rudy Buckhardt and John Ashbery, Black Mountain and Brackhage/Anger, the poetics of Maya Deren etc) are all well documented…however, a lot more digging needs to be done in order to reach experimental film and poetry interacting in the UK. Do you think this is because 'English Cinema, which Truffaut claims (with some justification) does not exist' (from* **Downriver***, 1991) or that simply, far less vocal attention has been paid to these interactions – and they do, in pockets, exist? Were there parallel conductors of chaos in lens and light?*

IS

There were jealous interconnections between the various practices, and far less pigeonholing (as you see from Jeff Nuttall's *Bomb Culture* [Note: I was reading this at the time of interview]) about where poetry puts up its border fences against film, or performance, or event. This was partly a matter of available venues and outlets. And partly a matter of funding. Only the requirement to solicit some derisory support separated the disciplines. Bureaucracies evolve around the horror of the commissioning process: random personalities or committees set up to make work conform to approved cultural categories. The era defined as the Art of the Proposal. Outside this hideous viral growth, now long past its critical point, there was very little division between film and poetry. A sharp operator like Peter Whitehead was able to identify the Albert Hall poetry readings of 11 June 1965 (chaotic, confused, but ripe for exploitation) as a breakthrough, a period defining event. Whitehead used accidental documentary coverage as a tool for marketing the legend of *Wholly Communion* as a book as well as a film. You had to wait for the years of VHS and then DVD to have the equivalent of book publication.

Probably *The Falconer*, a film I made with Chris Petit for Channel 4, covers my attempt to excavate meaning from the argument between film, poetry, myth-making and paranoia. It was possible in the Nineties to interrogate archival footage at the same time as shooting afresh, with the most casual means, and drawing in figures like Kathy Acker and Stephen Rodefer, who happened to be passing through London at the period of editing.

DS

*One particular film/poetry conversation that emerged in grow-
ing collaboration, between screen and page and between poet-
ry, bookselling, eccentricity, obscurity and memory, has grown
between you and Chris Petit in the loose trilogy of TV films
made for Channel 4:* **The Cardinal and the Corpse** *(1992),*
The Falconer *(1998) and* **Asylum** *(2000). Apart from* **The
Cardinal and the Corpse,** *which is now miraculously marooned on
Youtube, the other two are near impossible to track down...
much like the 'reforgotten' cast of characters, names, books,
poets and authors that double, echo and disappear in the
trilogy, the films themselves are now rumoured sightings in the
conjecture of memory and archive...this observation has already
been made (with more eloquence) by Stewart Home (***'Shamen
of Discontent and the Mirror People: A Detective Story in
Four Acts',*** *2000). Could you say a bit about the process of
collaborating with Chris Petit? Writers and poets (like Kathy
Acker and Ed Dorn) appear throughout, but were there any
particular filmic reference-points that inspired you and Chris?*

IS

I was lucky to come across Chris Petit at just the moment when
it was feasible, a brief interlude of accidental permissions, to
find commissions to make films with the adequate editing
time (and the technology) that would only have been allowed
previously for book publication. I wasn't really reading *Time Out*
at the period when Petit was film editor, but when I did come
across his pieces I enjoyed them. I thought he had good taste (it
agreed, in so many ways, with my own). And he wrote well, in a
clear and pared-down prose – with attitude (and glints of Ballard
and Manny Farber). The notable Petit feature film, *Radio On*, was
released in the same year, 1979, as my endgame collection, *Suicide
Bridge*. To say nothing of the arrival in Downing Street of Mrs
Thatcher.

I took the trip to Haverstock Hill to see *Radio On*. The
whole experience felt like time travel, like so many journeys
across so many cities in the Sixties and early Seventies. The film
was haunting but posthumous, German independent cinema
transposed to an English landscape – with a canny jukebox

soundtrack. Even at that time, my pleasure in the control displayed by the director, and several moments that equal anything in British cinema, was tinged with a certain melancholy. The skies are falling in. The abiding Petit microclimate is justified alienation, the poetics of ennui promising darker days ahead. *Radio On* was as much an obituary to ambition as a forerunner of a new kind of place-based essay film. And, inevitably, Petit's exile (from commissions and, finally, England). When the calls were no longer being taken, there was Petit's theoretical *Museum of Loneliness* and a post-film cinema of one-off spectral performances.

My own post-poem poetry (all that ended with *Suicide Bridge*) was as a compiler of secondhand book catalogues. Petit, researching Soho for a proposed history that became a novel, *Robinson*, was a customer. We talked on the phone. In many ways, the phone was his natural medium. He could have written a better (screen)play about imaginary conversations than Cocteau.

I had some visibility, having moved into fiction and London explorations, and Chris had the slightly discounted glamour of having delivered four feature films and a TV Miss Marple: we got the gig. After *The Cardinal and the Corpse*, which really was an obituary of the bounty-hunting used-book trade and the re-forgotten writers who supplied it, Petit had decided to get clear of hired professionals and to do it all himself. We started to drive around, shooting through the window with the freedom of some crazed war-zone veteran, spraying tracer bullets at the landscape. I picked up my 8mm camera. Chris could re-film my footage from the wall of his Archway bunker. Any ambitions towards a Warhol factory or a Fassbinder nest of collaborators (as featured in *Robinson*) very soon floundered.

The Cardinal and the Corpse is of sentimental interest as the record of a submerged period, between Sixties bohemia and New Labour boosterism, through the metaphor of the book-trade (echoes of *White Chappell, Scarlet Tracings*). The best thing about it is the cast – this confirms your reference to *Conductors of Chaos* and also to *London, City of Disappearances*. A good number of our witnesses are now dead: Robin Cook (Derek Raymond), Alexander Baron, Emanuel Litvinoff, John Latham, Tony Lambrianou, Martin Stone, David Seabrook, Pat Goldstein. Mike Moorcock relocated to Texas (and a future appearance in *Asylum*). Alan Moore and Brian Catling, already respected figures among and beyond their peers, rose to new levels of prominence. But I'm glad the film can now be viewed.

I'm not quite sure why – questions of music rights, lack of interest from producers, and Chris's preference for letting the myth cook without easy access – but the more achieved pieces, *The Falconer* and *Asylum* have only emerged at random screenings. On the cusp of lockdown, *Asylum* was projected in a former postal warehouse in Brussels, to an audience of about fifteen. *London Orbital*, on a loop, was playing mute in the oval panel of a glass door. Petit approved: 'That's the ideal version.' Both those films drew on significant collaborators: Bruce Gilbert (sound-gleanings and drone-composition), Dave McKean (animations) and Emma Matthews as editor. And visual conscience. Emma's contribution was vital. She lived with the footage, revising and refining. To say nothing of being required to do sound-recording and play a part in *Asylum*. For this period, the subterranean methods of the Sixties resurfaced in a new form. I think we could have taken this push further, but it was too late. It was always too late. *Asylum* had a secondary title: *The Final Commission*.

I don't think we were drawing on any particular film references, but on all film references. A long dialogue – movie gossip and other topics, including football and food – as we travelled around. We did view Chris Marker's *Sans Soleil*. But we were just as taken with a category of unnoticed dump-bin films that had some indefinable quality that made them worth looking at, part of a more complex story involving accidents of funding and production. Films like Budd Boetticher's *A Time for Dying*.

I was moved, seeing *Asylum* again in Brussels, with the virus at the door, to watch and hear from Ed Dorn – even though, by the time we filmed him, he was quite frail and on heavy medication. Maybe that was the high point of the whole series, catching a glimpse of someone who could, in another place and time, have had a major film presence. Meanwhile, we can contemplate the *Abilene! Abilene!* screenplay – and imagine what Brakhage could have done with it.

DS

You wrote a short book on David Cronenberg's **Crash** *(BFI, 1999) which perhaps draws more on Ballard and the publishing* *history of the book than Cronenberg's (re)vision of the text...I was wondering if you could say a bit more about Cronenberg's vision of* **Naked Lunch**? *And also, whether, to return to the mention of Mario Bava in* **Lud Heat**, *you have ever taken much of an interest in the more psychotronic, bizarre horror or 'exploitation' genre films that litter the overlooked and dank alleys of cinema's underground? There is a point in* **Lud Heat**, *where you list Roger Corman alongside Scientology and Manson Hole Visions...this question, apologies, is bundling together without much clarity...so, to attempt a vague order: could you say a bit about the formative influence of Burroughs in relation to film, and whether you find much interest or inspiration in the more budget and bizarre 'exploitation' films that proliferated from the late 60s and through to the 80s of video nasties?*

IS

I think I covered my original take on genre, exploitation, Scientology, Manson, Howard Hughes in three places: the deranged polemic of 'The Horse. The Man. The Talking Head' from *Suicide Bridge* and the riff on Michael Reeves, as part of 'Cinema Purgatorio' in *Lights Out for the Territory* (1997). But most thoroughly in a favourite book that never achieved visibility: *70 x 70. Unlicensed Preaching: A Life Unpacked in 70 Films* (2014). Here was a record of well-wasted hours and a task laid on me to curate seventy films (one for each birthday). The notion came from Paul Smith, who had also been responsible, down the years, for fixing many unlikely performances, exhibitions, CDs and LPs. From *Subversion in the Street of Shame* (at the Bridewell Theatre) to *The House of the Last London* (Gallery 46, Whitechapel). *70 x 70* was handsomely designed by Slim Smith and copiously illustrated. I think it answers most of the film questions you have set me. And it's still available from King Mob.

I felt, as I suggested in the BFI *Crash* monograph, that it was always a mistake to try and deliver a mainstream translation of a work like *Naked Lunch*. You could employ a number of strategies in the spirit of the underground film poets already mentioned. One exemplary assemblage (with built-in obsolescence) was the film made by Stanley Schtinter (another Petit collaborator) around the personality and myths of Brion

Gysin. This was a set of fragments, never to be completed or given a definitive form, and reliant on obscure screenings, misinformation and the hit-and-run of commissioning politics. (Paul Smith was again a lurking magus.) I think I have a ghostly part somewhere in this madness. But, like the river, you'll never enter the same screening twice. I think Schtinter has got it right, as the last non-paying member of a comprehensively theoretical (and disbanded) underground. The last avant-garde.

I've written too much about Burroughs – *American Smoke* etc – to add anything fresh now. But he's always there, for sure. Like seasonal flu. The Tangerine Press reissue of *Blade Runner: A Movie* was the necessary starting gun for the present viral crisis. Burroughs, like Ballard, always wrote the future in the present tense, and unmasked the past as a set of cosmic conspiracies.

DS

I have to return to that breath-taking section from **Suicide Bridge***: 'THE HORSE. THE MAN. THE TALKING HEAD. (a note on Howard Hughes)'. This has to be one of the most feverish poetic incantations of American culture from a poet outside of America that I've ever encountered. The apocalyptic rhythms of Ginsberg's* **Howl** *slither into the visionary paranoia of Burroughs; a contagion of language and image, of persona, star, conspiracy and madness, plumbing the glamorous gutters of Kenneth Anger's* **Hollywood Babylon** *via Ed Dorn's* **Gunslinger***...it is an incredibly powerful piece. Can you remember the momentum of writing that piece? It feels so infectiously alive with ideas, breathlessly overrunning prose to poetry, to prose-poetry and a tacit dismissal of the need to distinguish or categorise. No time to stop for labels. Just the blurring of connections. Was the inspiration tied to research as poetry, in the watching of films and following leads? Or was there something very particular to the life of Howard Hughes that broke into that energy for you?*

IS

That Howard Hughes rant in *Suicide Bridge* was so much of a rush for me, voices drowning out other voices, that I knew it had to be the end of something. When I was asked at a local gathering, shortly after the book had been published, 'What comes next?' I said, without thinking: 'Nothing. That's it.' Which turned out, in some ways, to be true. That was the finish of a chapter and there was quite a gap, taken up with book-dealing and driving around the country, before I got my head ready for the next tentative start. After doing something to which a few people could relate, like *Lud Heat*, I always managed to push the next one towards areas in which nobody wanted to travel without protective masks. *Radon Daughters* following on from decent coverage for *Downriver* was much the same. Although a few smart or perverse readers – like William Gibson, Mike Moorcock, Alan Moore, and, later, China Miéville – offered support, maybe through the posthumous connection with William Hope Hodgson and *The House on the Borderland* (now reissued in a nice edition by Swan River Press in Dublin). But *Radon Daughters* has gone, one of the reforgotten.

The Hughes piece was one of those rare occasions when the dictation comes faster than you can take it down. I had no sense of a potential readership and that was never an issue: I let rip. The trigger had been various pulp accounts of Hughes and, of course, *Gunslinger* and Dorn's fabulous conceit of the 'Literate Projector'.

And get this
They can distort the Projector
so that the script Departs
from the film, in Front
....
The point is it has to be read
to be seen, and like if the accent
is so incomprehensible and hysterical
it can only be coming from inside
the cinerama of the 3rd Reich
youre just not supposed to hear it.

There are a few special feverish times when these pieces happen, very quickly, after years of slow cooking and scattergun reading. The Hawksmoor essay was a bit like that, in a freezing Dorset bedroom, gloves on, after the summer of gardening and sneezing in Wapping and Shadwell and Tower Hamlets.

And, more recently, when I had the commission from Mike Goldmark to visit the Capuchin catacombs in Palermo, to provide a text to sit alongside photographs taken by Ian Wilkinson. *Our*

Late Familiars has a more stuttering momentum, plenty of overlapping voices and elements (Greta Garbo, Brian Catling's *The Vorrh*, Roussel, Freud, Lucky Luciano), but long delay in coming to publication, tinkering on my part, and the sense of writing for somebody's else inspiration, hobbled the finished product. Paranoid-critical derangement isn't always available. Maybe it fades with age, in mirror image, as we become more susceptible to viral invasion.

DS

Towards the end of John Roger's documentary, **London Over-ground** *(2016), we encounter a kind of 'behind the scenes' footnote to Andrew Kötting's film,* **Edith Walks** *(2016), in which Andrew describes your conversational company on walks as 'contagious and inspiring'. Since* **Swandown** *(2012), you have been a constant presence in Andrew's films. Could you say a bit about how your collaborative relationship with Andrew has developed over time? How would you describe the difference between this and your films with Chris Petit? They seem to tap into very different energies. And also, does your involvement with these projects ever prompt the desire to return behind the camera and to make more of your own films (in line perhaps with* **Maggot Street** *or the* **Hackney 8mm Diary Films***)?*

IS

I think the story of the collisions and collaborations with Andrew has been told a number of times. I was asked to review *Gallivant.* I loved it. Kötting, making a Thames voyage film of his own, was persuaded to read *Downriver.* He didn't get on with it at all. Too many words. And in the wrong order. He melted a little when I read him a site-specific section, about disasters and drownings, as we pedalled around the Isle of Grain on a plastic swan. We coincided in St Leonards-on-Sea, began a conversation over several walks and fell into numerous projects. They felt like Saga Adventure Holidays for me. In good company. I bombarded Andrew with potential film ideas and he went his own way. He took up ventures I had cooked, unsuccessfully for years, like the Clare walk (after *Edge of the Orison*) and the return of Dilworth's whalebone box to the Isle of Harris. But the final shape of these films was all his own: Andrew just locked himself away in his hut, inside a sail-maker's loft, in Hastings. And cranked up the heating. And he layered sound. And nibbled at shape and structure. And raided archive. By email and in conversation, I made suggestions for him to ignore. The films with Chris Petit were authentic collaborations. We had pretty much equal authorship. With Kötting they are, finally, all his. But his crew, blistered and battered, come back for more. The payoff is that I've been able to exploit him as a louder than life caricature in my books.

The collaborative walks with John Rogers have been a sidebar to this. John is remarkably painless to work with, the technology never gets in the way. And he is so easy on both sides of the camera. In a civilised world, he'd be given his own TV channel.

[2020]

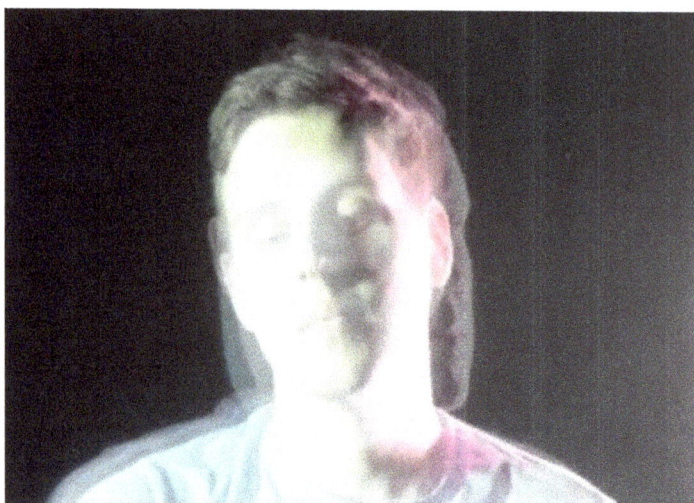

AARON KENT

The poetry of Aaron Kent is unpredictable, it swings from moments of lyric vulnerability into a feverish splintering of dream logic; it revises and revives itself until nervous compulsion becomes surreal convulsion; neither hesitant nor confrontational but itching uncomfortably in a volatility between, it is at once a fragile meshing of personal codes and the overarching socio-historical conditions that inform his cryptography of such meanings. Alongside his poetry, Aaron has also made experimental short films, written screenplays and founded the diverse and expanding poetry press, Broken Sleep Books. His work as an editor, like his poetry, has an energetically varied approach: welcoming poets from vastly differing aesthetic and thematic commitments into the same evolving momentum. It is a propulsive creativity that, however eclectic or unpredictable, braids into its growth returning strands. The constellation of reoccurring symbols, references and obsessions throughout Kent's ranging pamphlets begins to cultivate an unsteady tilt, a kind of unfinished cosmos that stares into its sleep-deprived reflection in the early hours to discover how much has changed, what is changing and, on moving back from the mirror – stepping onto the toes of another world in waiting – the possibility of another self, another space and time:

a place
amongst wasted noises
capillaries. Stairways
for astronomers,
leaking into the gaps
and waiting – O

(*from* 'Melatonin Spring Collection')

DS

I would like to open with a question relating to **The Rink** *(Dosto-yevsky Wannabe, 2018), it was my first introduction to your writing. I was excited by the busy collision of your themes, whereby the anxieties of nuclear war inhabit the anxieties of family – and both are brought into charged, almost gnomic,* *dialogue with a history of working class experience: how it filters through and fragments the poetics of a political stance, and equally, the politics of a poetic stance. What I loved was also how this book introduces a recurrent fascination in your work, the cumulative repetitions of constant revision, remembering and editing. For this all to be collaged over found texts, mirror texts, photocopied illustrations and scrawled drawing demonstrates the restless scope of what, for you and your readers, poetry can be. Whatever idea or topic is held by the poetic text is also slipping and turned over, returned to, in the stop and start of a sleepless imagination. A restless activity that ties into your own experiences of broken sleep and night terrors...and also, presumably, being the motivation behind titling your – increasingly expansive – poetry press, Broken Sleep Books. Your writing manifests this incredible complex of ideas, experience and formal energy, with a constant and vivid evocation of the visual: what is concealed and revealed becomes a rhythm of poetic seeing that draws together intimate psychology and historical violence as a kind of cinematic drama – a waking dream – played out in language. Could you say a bit about your own background in poetry and how your poetics & priorities have developed? At what point did you begin to connect a more filmic vocabulary and imagination to what you were doing in language?*

AK

I sucked at poetry for so long, like really was terrible. I wrote this one poem that was:

> *A drip drip dropping of emotional pain,*
> *A drip drip dropping of emotional rain,*
> *A drip drip dropping of reality's truth,*
> *A drip drip dropping of me to you.*

Like, how utterly terrible is that? And that wasn't even my worst. I was garbage, and it was because I didn't read poetry, or know poetry, and I was never taught it. That's kinda the thing though, when you're in some awful school near the bottom of the country school rankings, and the teachers are just hoping to get through the day, you ain't gonna be absorbing Donne or Plath or

Zephaniah, are you? I was so bored at college (where I took Film, English Lang/Lit, Law, Psychology) that I dropped out after less than a year. I worked in coffee shops and wrote garbage song lyrics on receipts when customers weren't in, and then I joined the Navy. I was lost and confused, and utterly aimless. So when I left the navy I drank and I kept things bottled up, and I decided to end it all by driving my car into a wall.

Eventually I got into university, I read more and I read better, and while I'm not certain I found my way there, I did find the beginning of the path, or the instructions on how to find my way. I decided to stop the slam stuff after a really scathing (and utterly correct) review. I decided I wouldn't write again until I had actually read. I read poetry, criticism, theory, journals, great novels, garbage novels, film scripts, children's books, non-fiction. And then I began writing again.

It wasn't until I started my MA in Film & TV that I connected filmic vocabulary. I was also working as a cinema projectionist at the time, and I learnt to absorb film in the same way I absorbed literature – to treat it with the same regard, to combine it.

DS

Could you say a bit about your research, as collaged in **The Rink**, *of the iconic Japanese Kaiju films and the transition of Gojira into Godzilla through American Cinema? The cultural and social movement between countries and what is saved, smuggled through or left behind runs throughout your poetry; are there particular poets or filmmakers that inspire you when addressing the traversal of social, geographical and cultural change?*

AK

My BA dissertation was about Godzilla, and how American cinema had taken a metaphor that represented the trauma they had inflicted, and cashed in on it. Essentially Gojira is representative of the bombs dropped on Hiroshima and Nagasaki. I remember reading a comparison in that it would be like Al-Qaeda making a blockbuster film about 9/11. Now, that's a bit of a reach, but the idea that America has profited off the suffering it caused is clear. The monster comes onto terra firma and destroys the city, but there are deeper moments in there – such as a mother cradling her children, telling them they'll see their father soon. The final weapon that can stop Gojira is liable to cause more damage if it falls into the wrong hands: humanity. So there arises a 'fight fire with fire' situation, in that, as Chon Noriega states, the monster created by the bomb requires the bomb to kill the monster.

I've been reading a lot of translation recently, and am particularly enjoying the work of Szilárd Borbély, how memory and trauma are interlinked and play off each other. I question my memories, because they're films in themselves. Have I changed the plot? Did the cast shift in time? How do I know the narrative is true? These things make up the bulk of our character, and who we are but we have no certainty that there is truth in our personal truth. But, if somebody just outside of the frame, or some-body catching a different part of the sentence were to report the memory it would take on a different shape – but still bear the same burden of truth as my reportage.

DS

The way in which you constantly connect elements of Hungarian history with the UK and, specifically, Cornwall, speaks to the way in which your poetry often collapses the historical into the psychological. The past of your family background and the futurity of family in becoming a father yourself seem always to be embedded in, and woven through, the turbulence and change of wider socio-historical events. Could you say a bit about how the personal and historical inhabit one another in your poetry...and what, throughout that exchange, is the significance of memory?

AK

I guess the personal and historical have always been at the core of who I am. I've tried to escape some horrific things that have happened to me, and I've failed. But in that failing I've found that I am able to shape how I perceive it and how I demonstrate it. At RASAC group therapy I finally learnt that forgiving myself is just as important, as cliché as that sounds, and when I let go of the pain and guilt and shame I felt about me, I was able to move forward.

I remember this one counsellor set up a chair and told me that my child self was sat in the chair, and I hated it, and I hated me as a child, and I wanted to swear at him and shout at him and I think I just cried. I never went back.

I also feel that personal/historical is so laden with identity. My dad is from London, and his family too, my Mum is from Bristol, but I'm from Cornwall. Am I Cornish? No, because the Cornish like it to be generational. But I identify as Cornish, up until last year it was the only home I knew. I lived it, and loved it, and was raised by Cornwall, more so than some people who moved as young kids. Then my Bampy is a war refugee from Hungary. I'm very working-class so how does that affect who I am? The working-class have been historically trampled underfoot. All of these things that make me who I am are the combination of historical influences and my personal identification. Where do I start with exploring that through poetry?

DS

I was thinking also about the sense of a growing cycle and recycling of words and images that appear, with conscious repetition, throughout **The Rink, St Day Road** *(BSB, 2018),* **Tertiary Colours, A Post-Traumatic Verse** *(KFS, 2018), and* **Melatonin Spring** *(Invisible Hand Press, 2020). The thread and fray of imagery around angels, moths, the moons of Saturn, Kintsugi and Tin mines; or the repetition of elements of a kind of cryptic personal language (further explored in the publication,* **Blood Fjord 89**, *Glyph Press) – like the never far-away utterance of 'Pikkatrap'. In* **St Day Road**, *as part of the book's opening explanation for its constraint-based methodology ('BLOOD FJORD '89 MANIFESTO', like a poetic allusion to Film's equivalent, 'Dogme '95 Manifesto' written by the Danish filmmakers, Lars Von Trier and Thomas Vinterberg), you stipulate: 'poems must call back to other poems by the writer'. It seems as if you are, throughout these chapbooks, creating a personally constellated poetic vision (at once psyche and historical cosmos), something that is unto itself, the vocabulary of enigmatic memory and connection. Has this approach, of calling back and linking between, always been central to your writing?*

There's a couple of things that moved me towards both the manifesto and the desire to call back to myself. Dogme '95 was an inspiration, the desire to remove optical filters, to use hand-held cameras, 35mm film – it felt like a real response to technology (sometimes) causing an alienation from a creative's work. That's not a 'back in my day' jab as technology has so many wonderful uses, but it is interesting to see how practice changes when the creative changes their approach to the work. With BLOOD FJORD '89 MANIFESTO, how does it affect your work if you can't leave the desk while typing? If you force yourself to have X amount of drafts? If you have to allow the mistakes their space on the paper? It changes the way you devise compared to Microsoft Word where you come and go, redraft without saving previous drafts, and delete mistakes without a second thought. You find yourself attached to the work in a different way, your body becomes essential to the creation in the same way as the words, or art, or images. Space, both personal and temporal, is a part of the process in a more conscientious way, and the act of creation becomes as concrete as what is produced.

The other thing to inspire me, particularly with calling back, is the band *The Wonder Years*. I'm not a mega fan, but I really like a lot of their work. They have a very clearly defined habit of re-using lyrics from songs from previous albums, or previous tracks on the same album, and slightly changing them to consider the difference since the writing. Like, they had a song 'Me vs the Highway', which was a B-side on their best album, *Suburbia I've Given You All and Now I'm Nothing*, in which Soupy sings about dreaming of car crashes. Then on *The Greatest Generation*, Soupy sings 'the highway won' on the track 'Passing Through a Screen Door'. And later, on the album *No Closer To Heaven*, Soupy sings about those same car crash dreams on the track 'A Song for Patsy Cline'. So, we aren't just listening to his life in that moment, we're looking back to where he's been, how he's changed, who he was against who he is. This is how to build a body of work – a living, breathing artefact in which the artist is responding to the artist, and allowing the audience in on a more private level. I want readers to read my poetry and find a line they recognise, and then to go back and follow a trail to the very core of this thing. To be able to unravel the thread with me. (I also read an interview with

Soupy where he mentioned how he puts real people's names in, real friends of his, because that's part of the intimacy of his writing – allowing others in on a deeper level.)

I have to ask you about the relationship between your experience of sleep and the way in which you write your poetry. Mentions of what sound like a truly punishing and disorientating difficulty with sleep, exist in many of your poems, and the title of your latest chapbook, **Melatonin Spring Collection***, refers to a natural hormone produced in sleep that, following the birth of your children, seems to be (thankfully) in a kind of awakening 'spring'. Elsewhere, a half-conscious state and an unnerving world of dream become the porous climates for an often-nightmarish Surrealism in your poetry. In the extraordinary, confrontational and hallucinatory long poem,* **Tertiary Colours***, trauma and memory open themselves up to an incredibly raw cinema of expression. I feel 'cinema' is a helpful metaphor as, like 'Cesare' the somnambulist in* **The Cabinet of Caligare** *(dir. Robert Weine, 1920) or Dante in first full-length Italian feature film,* **L'Inferno** *(1911), both of which are referenced in* **St Day Road***, there is a natural link between the underworld(s) of the unconscious and the sleepwalking landscapes of cinema. The Surrealists imagined entering the dark auditorium as a kind of wilful sleep; the projected image of film is the light in the dark, the movement of a dream. Could you say a bit about the relationship between sleep and poetry and then also sleep and cinema...do you ever find yourself watching films, writing or reading in times when you cannot sleep? Are there any filmmakers / films or poets/poetry that you feel also cover this atmosphere or experience in ways that provide solace, or perhaps something that chimes with your own experiences?*

Sleep has always been this elusive thing in my life, this far-away orb that I can't quite ever fully connect with. I have had night terrors my entire life, and when they were at their worst (five to ten times a night, every night for months), I kinda had this daze where sleep and reality never fully slipped into the other. So

I was always on the periphery of both, which lead to some depersonalisation, which lead to a whole boatload of other stuff.

But yeah, I'm getting there. *Melatonin Spring Collection* was an attempt to create a series of poems where the poems elude meaning in the way I eluded sleep. Sort of. I didn't want there to be words that could anchor it to reality, so any connectives had to muddy things further, rather than clarify, etc.

With film, Laurel & Hardy and Godzilla are the things that remind me of sleep the most. My Bampy loves Laurel & Hardy, and we'd fall asleep watching it whenever I stayed with him. To this very day sleep is still this enchanted black & white movie – that's not to say I don't dream in colour, rather that the act of sleeping sings to me in slapstick tones, in nostalgic theatre, in moonshine and harvest moons. Godzilla also became this beacon of escape in the lonely hours, the clash of cultural metaphor with increasingly outrageous farce was always so sublime. But mostly I just wanted to watch a giant monster crush buidings.

I have this recurring dream about Godzilla. The Big G comes along and starts crushing town, starting with a Tesco usually, and while most people run and scream and panic I do everything I can to get closer. I'm like this giddy child, and I just want to be there in the epicentre of Gojira.

I guess the obvious stuff would be like Aronofsky, but I felt *Paterson* (dir. Jim Jarmusch, 2016) was a really good evocation of life. I know sleep didn't play a huge part, but it had the feel of comfort, of warmth, of being at peace in this whole world built around a bus driver, and I adored that. *Synecdoche New York* (dir. Charlie Kauffman, 2008) chimes with the restless creativity produced by my ADHD combined with sleep, and the inability to relax as there's always the next thing to be doing. Michel Gondry is great at evoking sleep and dreams, and he does so in a way that others can't quite get right. Dreams aren't messages in a very realistic way, they don't follow a narrative, they slip and slide and change and twist, and most films/tv shows don't do this – they make dreams clear and concise. *Adventure Time* nails this too.

DS

Alongside your book, **Bampy** *(Hesterglock Press, 2018), which links the life of your Grandfather and the turbulence of the Budapest uprising of 1956, you created a series of short* *films that manipulate the hauntings of old news-reel footage with experimental audio. Could you say a bit about these films? The ghost layering of superimposition makes montage a kind of spectral palimpsest…and this movement is also at play in your short film,* **Yesterday I Forgot How To Spell My Name For A Minute And It Scared Me A Little***…which feels like a modest City Symphony…like a Town Chorus? a perambulating blur of Redruth (Cornwall) and some of the oppressive banalities of working class experience. Were there any filmmakers that particularly helped inspire these, or that you feel are related to their aesthetics/content?*

AK

With the *Bampy* short films, I wanted to connect the exodus of Cornwall with the exodus of Hungary, but, more specifically, my grandfather being forced from his home and his country, and connect that to me finding a home in him. The videos attempt to lace the events of the 1956 uprising, with the working-class redundancies of the Cornish mining industry. The audio was made using my daughter's playmat. It had like 7 keys that would make farmyard noises, or basic piano noises, when any pressure was applied to them. So for some of the films I used a single note and warped it, others I played a small ditty and messed with it. There's a sort of nod to Aphex Twin in that, who is from Redruth as well.

When I made these I was working as a media studies teacher at Truro college, and found that the markers/department heads wanted the students' work to be as clean and crisp as possible. So, while some of the students were making these great, retro, VHS style films, they'd be told to digitise it, and remove the analogue traces. I hated that. I wanted them to look at the works of Mark Jenkin, for example, and how to develop film. How to edit analogue into digital, and how to create in the moment with what you have available. That's what *Yesterday I Forgot…* particularly tries to examine; I was out, and I made something.

DS

You also studied for an MA in Film and TV, and have worked in scriptwriting (with one of your screenplays being adapted for the short, **Janaaza,** *in 2018). You mentioned a bigger more*

Hollywood-orientated screenplay that you eventually pulled the plug on? This sounds like quite a departure for an experimental UK Poet...could you talk more about your interest in writing for film and these recent experiences?

AK

The whole Hollywood stuff was a real exhausting time, creatively. I had interviewed a screenwriter (who I still really like, and occasionally email), and he and I got on well. I sent him a short film and he was really effusive in his praise for how I write dialogue in particular. I just kinda read the words in my head and respond how I'd respond, rather than respond to further the story – the story is gonna move along regardless, you don't need the characters to overtly usher it. Anyway, he wanted me to write a feature film, so I wrote a script of the Ray Bradbury short story *Dark they were, and Golden Eyed.* The problem was, I stuck to the short story too closely, so the dialogue was stilted. So they asked me to come up with my own thing and I wrote *Charlie (AKA The Elvis Presley Roadside Museum).* Oliver is two weeks away from becoming a father with his partner, his relationship with his dad, Stanley, is close to breaking point. Stanley drinks a lot. Oliver decides for them to have one last shot at reconciling or Stanley can never see his grandson, so they go to an old time, B-movie, slapstick convention. So, after like twenty-five minutes, everybody you see on screen is dressed as Laurel and Hardy or Mae Whitman or Buster Keaton. There's a lot more to it than that, but that's the basic premise.

They loved it, but wanted some changes. I made those changes. They loved it, felt it was the sorta film you'd enter into awards, but wanted some changes. I made those changes. They loved it, compared it to *Little Miss Sunshine*, but wanted changes. I made those changes. They wanted, then, for me to try and write a new screenplay to give *Charlie* some breathing room. so I wrote a 40 page outline. They loved it but wanted changes. This went on until I just couldn't do it anymore. I hadn't been given an option, I had made no money, and it had been a couple years. Plus my other creative work had been suffering. So I stopped, and I decided I'd turn them into novels instead.

Your poetry has encompassed early success in the Slam world and your current more experimental page poetry, and this has drawn into its orbit: invented language, collage, constraints, hallucinatory investigations of memory and history, and a more emotive immediacy that veers between confrontational anguish and vulnerable candour. Has the presence of film, screenplays and script been a recent development, or has this interest always informed your writing? How do you imagine the relationship between film and poetry might change or progress in your practice?

AK

I sucked as a slam poet – I was so cheap, and lazy, and just going for easy emotion rather than anything with depth. I hadn't read around the work I was creating I hadn't bothered to research anything. I just chucked words on the page, didn't bother editing, and hoped people would skip along the many, many gaps. I cannot express enough how bad I was.

I was interested and invested in screenwriting before poetry and prose. I took film studies at A level and dropped out after a year, but found myself entranced by the films I'd been introduced to. Films such as *Cinema Paradiso* (dir. Giuseppe Tornatore, 1988) . I, eventually, decided to take a shot at screenwriting and wrote a weird, little short film about a guy who become obsessed with James Dean. His relationship breaks down as he finds himself becoming less an impersonation, and more an embodiment. It ends with him spending his nights driving down the wrong side of roads, hoping to emulate Dean's final moments. I didn't do anything with it.

I have been working on a project with another poet – a poetry book that takes the form of a screenplay. We take it in turns to write pages, and the narrative, therefore, is shaped by what the other person wrote previously. This way I can no longer determine how, or where, I want to guide things without leaving that up to somebody else's whim. It has been a fascinating project, and I am incredibly interested in where it goes, and if it would ever be filmable (I think not).

I want to write poetry like that shot in Gus Van Sant's *Elephant* (2003) where the guy walks across campus for like 3 minutes and nothing really happens. We just watch him walk. Like a field recording, I guess. That's what I want to do at the moment; evoke the filmic mundanity of life.

I do, though, see myself as a fraudster. Not imposter syndrome – a full-on fraudster. With my first book *Subsequent Death*, it's just a bunch of typographical stuff with absolutely no substance. It's weak. I'm certain *The Rink* was accepted because of all the stuff around the poems – like, if I were to send those poems anywhere by themselves they wouldn't be accepted. I almost literally papered over the glaring cracks in my work. *St Day Road* is ten poems with the edits of each poem, and I published it with BSB, so there's no arbiter of quality (clearly). I've always felt *The Last Hundred* was more about William Arnold's photos than my poems, my poems just gave these glorious photos some marginalia. And I don't think any of the nakjarnorkiman poems would be published if they weren't half in a made-up language, it covers the inadequacy of the poems.

DS

A huge part of your creativity must have changed with the founding and editing of your wonderful press, Broken Sleep Books. What was it that compelled you to start the press and do you conceive of publishing as a creative venture in line with your own poetic values and aesthetics? It seems that your expanding list includes a very diverse range of work, from emergent poets to J.H. Prynne (please say a bit about the experience of that publication!) and valuing the need for an inclusivity across differing writing backgrounds. What kind of writing are you keen to support with BSB and has this changed at all since starting the press? I also wanted to say a huge CONGRATULATIONS!! to the initiative you started around Black Lives Matter (creating a raffle of BSB books that was then inundated with the enthusiasm of other donations) raising £5,364…this was such a heartening moment, to see UK small presses working together with such strong intent and community. I think that, and the Ignota reading(' **Break Into the Forbidden'**), *gave some real hope for the positive work to come in support of BLM in UK poetry.*

I'd read a couple manuscripts which I loved, but which weren't getting traction elsewhere. So I started BSB to publish those books that I felt deserved a readership, and should be read. Then the press grew from there. Initially I conceived of publishing pamphlets in cassette cases, and collections in VHS cases, but that was too costly and not at all efficient. I have this laserdisc, *Curse II: The Bite* (dir. Frederico Prosperi as 'Fred Goodwin', 1989) it's a German sequel and my laserdisc is in Japanese. It's about this person that gets bitten by a snake, and then their arm becomes a snake. Its trash. But the cover is a fantastically B-movie cover, and I wanted poetry books that had that sort of style. Which has changed immensely as I'm all about minimalism now!

I try not to publish something with profit in mind, that's not why I do this. I want to publish because that are deserving of a great readership, and that's regardless of financial gain. I also try (try) to not allow my poetic preference to take precedence. I want to publish books that are brilliant, or have the potential to be brilliant, and not just books that are my exact taste.

I got to know Jeremy [Prynne] a few years back over email, and we kept in contact since. We send each other our newest releases, chat back and forth, and he even handwrote me a letter. I'd always wanted to publish him but knew Broken Sleep wasn't limited enough, so when I started Legitimate Snack I just had to enquire. He emailed back within a week with the book, each poem typed in the body of a separate email. He was really easy to work with!

DS

And now, in time-honoured and unimaginative fashion, I'd like to end by asking you what poetry you have read, or have been reading, recently that has excited you? And, naturally, to extend the obligatory question…. have you seen any films recently that have particularly inspired, confused, or entertained you?

I've just moved and put all my books out, after they've been in boxes for two months, so I'm diving into poetry books on a whim: Walt Whitman, Alice Oswald, a bunch of surrealism, Spenser, Gillian Clarke, Mary Jean Chan, a bit of Blake, Roger Robinson. I read a lot of fiction too, and have really enjoyed *The Loney* by Andrew Michael Hurley, *The Nickel Boys* by Colson Whitehead, and *Saltwater* by Jessica Andrews. Chris Ware's graphic novels are a perfect mix of film and literary fiction, as are Adrian Tomine's.

I haven't had much of a chance with film recently, as having a 6-month-old and a 3-year-old means I absorb *Peppa Pig* more than anything else. But Rue has enjoyed *Adventure Time* recently, which is great for me because it's fantastic – it is so enchanting and gets that wonderful mix of humour that works for both kids and adults. It's incredibly forward thinking, it doesn't push stereotypes, and it showcases the joy in adventure regardless of who you are.

I am interested in films of field recordings at the moment, life carrying on, the routines we don't even notice. My Bampy watches this film of people going to work at the turn of the 20th century. I think it was one of the first pieces of footage ever recorded, and watching these people just going about their day, the same monotony as now, fascinating.

Acknowledgements

I would first and foremost like to thank all of the wonderful contributors whose generosity, in their art and conversation, continue to be a source of inspiration. Special thanks to Andrew Kötting for his supportive correspondence, and for the kind provision of his photo for the front cover. To family, friends and collaborators – thank you. Finally, I'd like to extend my sincere gratitude to Aaron Kent and Broken Sleep.

LAY OUT YOUR UNREST